福建省文化和旅游厅　组织编写

编著
苏西

翻译
陈小慰

图片
康伦恩
白桦
林乔森
陈亚元
杨戈
子健传媒 等

福建的世界遗产

World Heritage Sites in Fujian

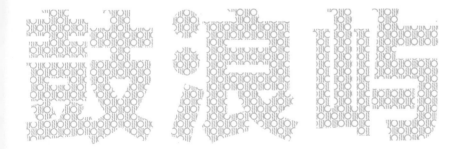

鼓浪屿

Kulangsu

海峡出版发行集团
THE STRAITS PUBLISHING & DISTRIBUTING GROUP

福建人民出版社
FUJIAN PEOPLE'S PUBLISHING HOUSE

图书在版编目（CIP）数据

鼓浪屿：汉英对照 / 苏西编著；陈小慰译．--福州：
福建人民出版社，2020.5（2021.10 重印）
（福建的世界遗产）
ISBN 978-7-211-08315-2

Ⅰ.①鼓… Ⅱ.①苏… ②陈… Ⅲ.①鼓浪屿—地方
史—汉、英 Ⅳ.①K295.73

中国版本图书馆 CIP 数据核字（2019）第 288403 号

鼓浪屿
GULANGYU

作　　者：苏　西
翻　　译：陈小慰
责任编辑：周跃进
美术编辑：陈培亮
装帧设计：［澳］Harry Wang
内文排版：良之文化传媒
图片支持：厦门子健文化传媒公司
出版发行：福建人民出版社　　　　　电　　话：0591-87533169（发行部）
网　　址：http://www.fjpph.com　　电子邮箱：fjpph7211@126.com
地　　址：福州市东水路 76 号　　　　邮政编码：350001
经　　销：福建新华发行（集团）有限责任公司
印　　刷：雅昌文化（集团）有限公司
地　　址：深圳市南山区深云路 19 号
开　　本：787 毫米×1092 毫米　　1/16
印　　张：14.75
字　　数：324 千字
版　　次：2020 年 5 月第 1 版
印　　次：2021 年 10 月第 2 次印刷
书　　号：ISBN 978-7-211-08315-2
定　　价：88.00 元

目 录

Contents

01

世遗档案

UNESCO's Introduction to Kulangsu

◎ 鼓岛夜曲。（朱庆福 摄）
Kulangsu at night. (Photo by Zhu Qingfu)

名　　称：鼓浪屿：历史国际社区
列入时间：2017年7月被正式列入《世界遗产名录》
遗产类型：世界文化遗产

遗产价值

　　鼓浪屿位于福建九龙江入海口，与厦门岛隔海相望。随着1843年厦门开辟为通商口岸和1903年鼓浪屿成为国际社区，这座位于中国南方海岸线上的小岛突然成了中外交流的重要窗口。鼓浪屿是中西文化交流融合的特例。鼓浪屿有机的城市肌理清晰地保留了其发展变化的痕迹，见证了数十年间多元文化不断融入当地文化的过程。岛上拥有包括传统闽南建筑、西方古典复兴建筑和殖民地外廊式建筑等不同的建筑风格。从鼓浪屿兴起的厦门装饰风格融合了20世纪早期的现代风格和装饰艺术，是对文化间影响融合最突出的证明。

◎ 俯瞰三一堂。（林乔森 摄）
Bird's eye view of Trinity Church. (Photo by Lin Qiaosen)

◎ 黄家花园中楼。（黄恒日 摄）
Central building of Huang Family Villa.
(Photo by Huang Hengri)

Kulangsu, a Historic International Settlement

Inscribed in July, 2017 on the World Heritage List

Cultural Property

Kulangsu (also known as Gulangyu) is a tiny island located on the estuary of the Jiulongjiang (Chiu-lung) River, opposite the city of Amoy (now Xiamen). With the opening of a commercial port at Amoy in 1843, and the establishment of the island as an international settlement in 1903, this island off the southern coast of the Chinese empire suddenly became an important window for Sino-foreign exchanges. Kulangsu is an exceptional example of the cultural integration that emerged from these exchanges, which remains woven into its urban fabric. There is a mixture of different architectural styles including the traditional South Fujian Style, Western Classical Revival Style and Veranda Colonial Style. The clearest testimony to this fusion of various stylistic influences is a new architectural movement, the Amoy Deco Style, which is a synthesis of the Modernist Style of the early 20th century and Art Deco.

入选理由

鼓浪屿位于福建省厦门市九龙江入海口，与厦门岛隔着600米宽的鹭江海峡。随着1843年厦门开辟为通商口岸和1903年鼓浪屿成为国际社区，这座位于中国南方海岸线上的小岛突然成了中外交流的重要窗口。鼓浪屿现留存有931座展现本土和国际不同风格的历史建筑、园林和自然景观、历史道路网络，体现了现代人居理念和当地传统文化的融合。

◆ 通过当地华人、还乡华侨以及来自多个国家的外国居民的共同努力，鼓浪屿发展成为具有突出文化多样性和现代生活品质的国际社区，也成为活跃于东亚和东南亚一带的华侨、精英的理想定居地，体现了19世纪中叶至20世纪中叶的现代人居理念。

◆ 鼓浪屿是文化间交融的一个特例。鼓浪屿有机的城市肌理清晰地保留了其发展变化的痕迹，见证了数十年间多元文化不断融入原有文化的过程。从鼓浪屿兴起的新建筑运动——厦门装饰风格是对这一文化间影响融合最突出的证明。

◆ 鼓浪屿的建筑特色和风格体现了中国、东南亚和欧洲建筑与文化价值观和传统的交融，这种交融的产生得益于岛上居住的外国人和归国华侨的多元性。岛上建立的聚落不仅反映了定居者从原籍地或先前居住地带来的影响，还混合形成了一种全新的风格——厦门装饰风格。厦门装饰风格产生于鼓浪屿，其影响力覆盖了东南亚沿海地区乃至更远的地方。就此而言，鼓浪屿见证了亚洲全球化早期各种价值观念的交汇、碰撞和融合。

◆ 鼓浪屿是厦门装饰风格的起源地和杰出代表，这种风格以厦门在本土闽南方言中的称呼Amoy命名，指的是首先在鼓浪屿岛上出现的建筑风格和类型，体现了当地建筑传统灵感与来自西方早期建筑风格灵感的融合，特别是现代主义和闽南移民文化的影响。基于上述因素，厦门装饰风格体现了传统建筑类型向新形式的转型。鼓浪屿反映了东南亚地区的建筑从传统的地方风格向现代主义和国际化过渡。

◎ 天风海涛鼓浪屿。（林乔森 摄）
Kulangsu in between the sky and the sea. (Photo by Lin Qiaosen)

Outstanding Universal Value

Kulangsu is located on the estuary of Chiu-lung (the Jiulongjiang) River opposite the city of Amoy across the 600-meter-wide Lujiang Strait. With the opening of Amoy as a commercial port in 1843, and Kulangsu as an international settlement in 1903, the island off the southern coastal areas in the Chinese empire suddenly became an important window for Sino-foreign exchanges. Its heritage reflects the composite nature of a modern settlement composed of 931 historical buildings in a variety of local and international architectural styles, natural scenery, and historic gardens surrounded by a historic network of roads.

◆ Through the concerted endeavour of local Chinese, returned overseas Chinese, and foreign residents from many countries, Kulangsu developed into an international settlement with outstanding cultural diversity and modern living quality. It also became an ideal dwelling place for the overseas Chinese and elites who were active in East Asia and South-eastern Asia as well as an embodiment of modern habitat concepts of the period between mid-19th and mid-20th century.

◆ Kulangsu is an exceptional example of the cultural fusion that emerged from these exchanges, which remain legible in an organic urban fabric formed over decades constantly integrating more diverse cultural references. The clearest testimony to this fusion of various stylistic influences is a genuinely new architectural movement featuring the development of the Amoy Deco Style, which emerged from the island.

◎ 20世纪30年代的鼓浪屿。（白桦 供图）
Kulangsu in the 1930s. (Courtesy of Bai Hua)

◆ Kulangsu exhibits in its architectural features and styles the interchange of Chinese, Southeast Asian and European architectural and cultural values and traditions produced in this variety by foreign residents or returned overseas Chinese who settled on the island. The settlement created not only mirrored the various influences settlers brought with them from their places of origin or previous residence but it synthesized a new hybrid style—the so-called Amoy Deco Style, which developed on Kulangsu and exerted influences over a far wider region in Southeast Asian coastal areas and beyond. In this regard, the settlement illustrates the encounters, interactions and fusion of diverse values during an early Asian globalization stage.

◆ Kulangsu is the origin and best representation of the Amoy Deco Style. Named after Xiamen's local Hokkien dialect name "Amoy", Amoy Deco Style refers to an architectural style and typology, which first occurred on Kulangsu and illustrates the fusion of inspirations drawn from local building traditions, early Western and in particular modernist influences as well as the South Fujian migrant culture. Based on these the Amoy Deco Style shows a transformation of traditional building typology towards new forms, which were later referenced throughout Southeast Asia and became popular in a wider region.

◎ 鼓浪屿的制高点日光岩。（康伦恩 摄）
Sunlight Rock: the point of the highest elevation on Kulangsu. (Photo by Kang Lun'en)

United Nations · World Heritage
Educational, Scientific and · Convention
Cultural Organization ·

CONVENTION CONCERNING
THE PROTECTION OF
THE WORLD CULTURAL
AND NATURAL HERITAGE

The World Heritage Committee
has inscribed

Kulangsu,
a Historic International Settlement

on the World Heritage List

Inscription on this List confirms the outstanding
universal value of a cultural or
natural property which requires protection for
the benefit of all humanity

DATE OF INSCRIPTION

12 July 2017

Irina Bokova

DIRECTOR-GENERAL
OF UNESCO

02

岛之风华

The Beauty of Kulangsu

○ 覆鼎岩上的郑成功塑像。（康伦恩 摄）
Statue of Koxinga (Zheng Chenggong) on
Fuding Rock. (Photo by Kang Lun'en)

◎ 日光岩上的"鼓浪洞天"石刻。（康伦恩 摄）
"Gu Lang Dong Tian" (Wonderland of Idyllic Beauty) inscribed on Sunlight Rock.(Photo by Kang Lun'en)

天风海涛——自然景观与文化遗迹

清代周凯所著的《厦门志》里这样描写这座小岛：

"鼓浪屿，厦门东南五里；在海中，长里许。上有小山、民居、田园、村舍（按《方舆纪要》：'在大嶝西，旧有民居。洪武二十年，悉迁内地；成化以后，渐复其旧'），郑氏屯兵于此（上有旧砦遗址）。左有剑石、印石浮海面，下有鹿耳礁、燕尾礁（《鹭江志》）。东为日光岩（亦曰晃岩。上有龙头石，俗名龙头山。池直夫居其下；有晃园，极花竹之胜），石刻"鼓浪洞天"四大字。有寺，乾隆间僧瑞琳募修（《县志》）；旧惟石室一间，后建高楼及旭亭。旁有小洞，堪避暑（《嘉禾名胜记》。今寺圮）。"

"鼓浪屿的形胜与自然的魅力在中国的海岸线上独一无二。大自然赋予它美丽、雄壮而粗犷。"曾经居住在鼓浪屿的外国人如此形容鼓浪屿。面积仅有1.88 平方千米的它，是巴金笔下"南国的梦"，是舒婷的"生命之源"，更是诗人蔡其矫比喻的"彩色的楼船"。多少人着迷于她的静谧美丽！经由窄窄的鹭江登临这座只能步行、毫无车马喧嚣的岛屿，便能体会为何百年前居住于此的传教士和外国人把它比喻为"尘世里的天堂"。

华屋大宅的门窗柱廊，教堂寺院的唱诗梵呗，摩崖石刻的风云激荡，草木植物的四季轮回，世家名人的悲欢离合，普通人家的岁月静好……穿越历史的烟尘，从几百年前的荒芜小岛到世界文化遗产，鼓浪屿的变迁更替，也许那些山岩礁石、海浪沙滩、洞窟井泉是最沉默也最忠实的见证者。在天风海涛之间，自然景观在历史的进程中拥有了特殊的内涵与折射，也成为这座岛屿的文化遗迹，串联起那些年代、故事与人物。它们是一曲恢宏壮阔又不失细腻绵长的交响乐，在岁月流逝之后仍未停止……

Paradise on Earth: A Collection of Natural and Cultural Wonders

Kulangsu has been an attraction to too many with Zhou Kai, an official and poet in the Qing Dynasty (1616—1911), remarking on the tiny island in his *Amoy Chronicles*:

"Kulangsu, some 2.5 kilometers southeast of Amoy, is an island with a length of a bit more than half a kilometer, on which there are hills, pastures and villages. According to geographical records, there were settlements on the island long time ago but residents moved further inland in 1387. People came back to live here again decades later after Ming Emperor Xianzong took the throne in around 1465. It used to be the site where Koxinga (Zheng Chenggong) stationed his troops and the remains of the former fort are still there. To the west, Sword Rock and Seal Rock stand above the surface of the sea, and to the south are Lu'er Reef and Yanwei Reef, based on *Lujiang Chronicles*. To the east is Sunlight Rock on which 'Gu Lang Dong Tian' (Wonderland of Idyllic Beauty) was inscribed. Near Sunlight Rock (also known as Huangyan Rock) is Longtou Rock (Dragon Head Rock) which sits upon Longtou Hill. Chi Zhifu, a well-known Ming Dynasty (1368—1644) scholar of South Fujian, used to live at its foot in Huangyan Garden where flowers and bamboos were abundant. It was also stated in *County Records* that there was a temple nearby which the monk Ruilin raised funds to build during the reign of Emperor Qianlong in the Qing Dynasty. According to *Places of Interest in Amoy* compiled by Huang Riji of the time, the temple started with only a stone hall and was later expanded to become a complex with buildings and pavilions. Next to the temple was a small cave which provided relief from the summer heat."

◎ 鹭江两岸，文化遗产与现代化城市的视觉反差。（王福平 摄）
Heritage buildings and a modern city: a clear contrast across the Lujiang Strait. (Photo by Wang Fuping)

"Nature endows Kulangsu with beauty, majesty and ruggedness not found anywhere else on the coast of China". These are the words of previous residents of Kulangsu. With an area of only 1.88 square kilometers, it has been dubbed the "dream of the south", "source of life" and a "kaleidoscopic ship" by renowned Chinese poets such as Ba Jin, Shu Ting and Cai Qijiao. Merely across the narrow stretch of the Lujiang Strait, it is easy to see why this tranquil island, which one may go around only by foot, attracts so many people. Away from the hustle and bustle of modern urbanization, it is easy to agree with the missionaries and foreigners who lived here 100 years ago who called it "Paradise on Earth".

The grand mansions and villas, churches and temples, cliff inscriptions and beautiful flora, as well as the joys and sorrows of people both ordinary and extraordinary... all these are borne witness to only by the rocks, reefs, waves, beaches, caves and springs. Over the years the natural features of Kulangsu have observed the activity of humankind, and today, they tell the story how Kulangsu evolved from a tiny island off the coast of Amoy to a World Cultural Heritage Site, and in the future, they will continue to tell this story for as long as the passage of time exists.

◎ 19世纪70年代的鼓浪屿。（白桦 供图）
Kulangsu in the 1870s. (Courtesy of Bai Hua)

"圆洲仔" 与渔民开岛

　　鼓浪屿，最初不过是个无人的小小荒岛，孤悬于茫茫大海中。因为形呈椭圆，鼓浪屿最初得名"圆洲仔"。"野人惊问客，此地只临鸥。归路应无路，十洲第几洲？"明代天启三年（1623），福建巡抚南居益的诗《鼓浪屿石岩礼佛同谢窹之池直夫》是留存下来的第一首关于鼓浪屿的古代诗文。诗文中描绘的正是彼时鼓浪屿的荒芜萧疏。

　　一直到数百年前的宋末元初，附近西边渔村的李姓渔民为躲避海上风浪，在岛上的西北部搭盖可以栖身的简易住所，他们久而定居，成了鼓浪屿最早的岛民。接着，又来了黄姓人家和洪姓人家，黄氏依山而居，洪姓临海筑屋。鼓浪屿逐渐形成了有岛民居住的三个渔耕村落：内厝澳、岩仔脚和鹿耳礁。

"Yuanzhouzi" (Round Sandbank) and Development of Kulangsu

Kulangsu used to be a desolate island just off the coast and was originally named "Yuanzhouzi" (Round Sandbank) after its oval shape. In a Ming Dynasty poem by Nan Juyi, then governor of Fujian, in memory of his meeting with Chi Zhifu, written in 1623, he described the wilderness: "Where is this place? Inhabited only by seabirds, there seems to be no return."

It was not until the late Song Dynasty around 1278 to 1279 and early Yuan Dynasty between 1271 and 1285 that a family of fishermen by the name of Li from a nearby village in the west built shelters on the northwest of the island and became the first settlers of Kulangsu. Then came the Huang family and the Hong family. The Huang family built their houses by the hills and the Hong family constructed their dwellings by the sea. Gradually, Kulangsu developed into a place inhabited by islanders of three fishing villages, namely Neicuo'ao, Yanzijiao and Lu'erjiao.

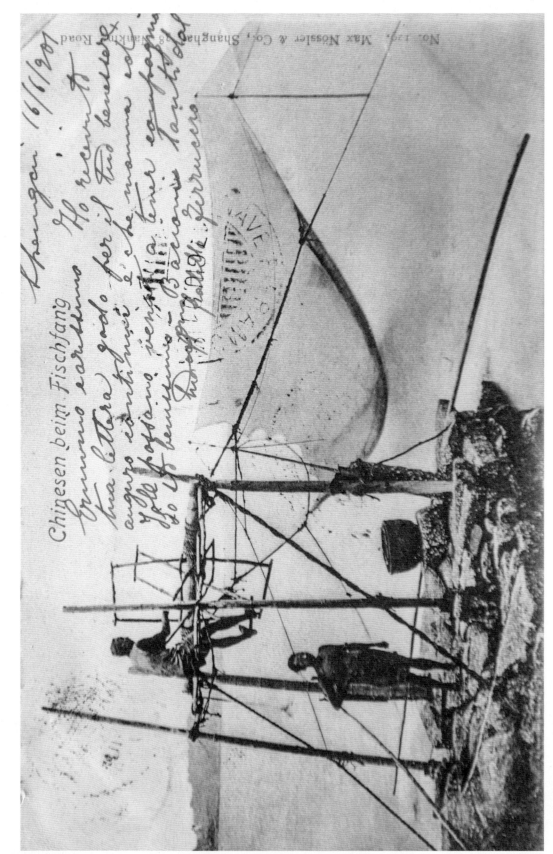

© 旧时鼓浪屿的渔民。（滕亚元 供图）
Fishermen of Kulangsu in old days. (Courtesy of Chen Yayuan)

Joss procession held at the Settlements, Kulangsoo, Amoy.

◎ 旧时鼓浪屿的游神活动。（陈亚元 供图）
A joss procession held on Kulangsu in old days. (Courtesy of Chen Yayuan)

　　随着渔民一起来到小岛上的，有"敬天公""敬土地"的民间习俗。居民为保生大帝建起宫庙——种德宫。如今存于岛上内厝澳的种德宫古榕掩映，幽静祥和，是传统的三门二进殿宇。除了保生大帝，种德宫还祀奉土地公、注生娘娘、虎爷及36官将的神像，护厝中还供奉着观音菩萨和关帝爷。种德宫一直延续着名目繁多、形式有趣的传统祭祀仪式，它是鼓浪屿原住民聚落的"重要成员"，亦是国际社区信仰包容性的体现。

　　还有几经迁徙，现在安身在鹿礁路林氏府一侧的兴贤宫，供奉的也是保生大帝。它曾是鼓浪屿上重要的信仰场所，出现在很多外国人的文字记录里。

◎ 种德宫。（杨戈 摄）
Zhongde Temple. (Photo by Yang Ge)

The fishermen brought with them to the island the religion customs of "Worship of God of Heaven" and "Worship of God of Earth". Zhongde (Virtue Cultivating) Temple, a temple complex worshipping the "Baosheng God" (Guardian of Health and Well-being) was built. Secluded in deep green of old banyan trees at Neicuo'ao, Zhongde Temple is a traditional three-gate and two-compound building. In addition to Baosheng God, the temple also enshrines statues of the God of Earth, Lady Zhusheng (Child-Giving Goddess), the God of Tiger (Guardian of the Neighborhood) and 36 gods of various other roles, as well as the Goddess of Mercy, and Kuan Ti (Guan Yu), the God of War in side halls. Zhongde Temple carried on various traditional sacrificial rituals, which not only makes it integral to the Kulangsu aboriginal community, but embodies the inclusive attitude towards religions on Kulangsu.

There is also Xingxian Temple which enshrines Baosheng God. Now located next to Lin Family Villa at today's Lujiao Road after several relocations, the temple was once a significant place of worship and appears in many foreign records.

同样被沿海人民所信奉的妈祖娘娘也随着渔民来到了鼓浪屿。岛上的天妃庙是最早祀奉妈祖的地方，后来一度成为佛教庵堂——瑞咣庵。据载，福建水师提督王得禄因为求得妈祖娘娘的眷顾，在海上打了胜仗，得以升迁发达。他在清朝嘉庆十八年（1813）重修扩建了瑞咣庵，改名为三和宫，为妈祖娘娘重起香火。王得禄将这个故事刻碑为铭，镌于三和宫后的摩崖绝壁上。《重兴鼓浪屿三和宫记》摩崖石刻幅高约11.5米，宽约6.4米，镌刻楷书17行，共346字。碑文由王得禄撰文，候补知县王圭璋书写，记载了三和宫重修始末并有王得禄镇压嘉庆年间海上武装集团头子蔡牵、朱濆武装起义等重要史实。这是目前国内所存最大的记述天妃妈祖的摩崖石刻，为福建省级文物保护单位。

A major deity along the coast, the legendary Sea Goddess Mazu also came to Kulangsu with the fishermen. The Temple of the Heavenly Goddess where Mazu was first worshipped on the island was converted into Ruiguang Nunnery. According to records, Wang Delu, Commander-in-chief of Fujian Navy, won a sea battle and got promoted by the grace of Mazu. To show his gratitude, he rebuilt and expanded Ruiguang Nunnery in 1813. He then renamed the convent Sanhe Taoist Temple, and rededicated it to Mazu. Wang Delu later had the story inscribed on the cliffs behind the temple. 11.5 meters high, 6.4 meters wide and totaling 346 characters across 17 lines, the inscription was drafted by Wang Delu himself and hand written by alternate Magistrate Wang Guizhang, which gave an account of the reconstruction of the temple, as well as the history of Wang Delu's suppression of the uprising of the maritime armed group led by Cai Qian and Zhu Fen. This is currently the largest cliff inscription regarding Mazu and is now under the protection of Fujian Provincial Government.

◎ 《重兴鼓浪屿三和宫记》摩崖石刻。（杨戈 摄）
Cliff Inscriptions about Sanhe Taoist Temple's Reconstruction. (Photo by Yang Ge)

礁石海滩镌刻的历史

　　鼓岛之一隅，有石在岸，常年累月被潮水冲刷出大洞，每逢潮涨，声如鼓浪，小岛因之更名为"鼓浪屿"。1878年，曾到鼓浪屿担任三年代理英国领事、后来的英国三大汉学巨匠之一的翟理斯，在他所著的《鼓浪屿简史》中写到"鼓浪屿"名字的来历："它之所以被称作'鼓浪屿'，乃由于海浪在其西北海岸某处发出一种特别像鼓的声音。"这是关于"鼓浪石"的传说第一次被记录于文字。

　　《鼓浪屿简史》还记载，岛上山岭蜿蜒的自然形态被一些西方人比喻为帆船，岛屿中部高耸的岩石被形容为桅杆。鼓浪屿工部局（1902年《厦门鼓浪屿公共地界章程》签订后，次年，作为公共地界管理机构的鼓浪屿工部局就在清政府的授权下成立了。管理职权涵盖了税收、治安、市政建设、公共卫生等。1945年鼓浪屿公共地界被国民党政府正式收回。）时期公布的《厦门鼓浪屿公共地界规例》还曾提出保护岛上印石（印斗石）、覆鼎石、升旗山石、鸡母石、鸡冠石、金冠石、燕尾石、骆驼山石、鼓浪石、日光岩等名胜岩石的要求。

◎ 日光岩上有历朝历代的摩崖石刻。（康伦恩 摄）
Cliff inscriptions of past generations on Sunlight Rock. (Photo by Kang Lun'en)

History as Told by Reefs and Beaches

Legend has it that there was a huge rock on the coast in which a hole was created by the constant erosion by waves. The stone would generate a sonorous sound like beating drums whenever the tide rose and water entered that hole. Thus the rock got its name "Drum Wave Rock" and the little island was renamed after it to become "Kulangsu" (the 3-character formation "Ku-lang-su" referring respectively to drum, tide and island). In 1878, Herbert Allen Giles, who had been British acting consul on Kulangsu for three years and later a well-known British sinologist, wrote a book entitled *A Short History of Koolangsu* in which he says, "The island was named 'Kulangsu' because tides somewhere near its northwest coast made a sound very much like the beating of drums." This is the first written record about the legend of Drum Wave Rock.

In the book, Giles also writes that the natural form of winding ridges on the island could be compared to ships and the towering rocks to masts. In 1902, *Land Regulations for the Settlement of Kulangsu, Amoy* was signed. And one year later the Kulangsu Municipal Council as the administrative body of the island was established under the authorization of the Qing government. Since then the Council had been in administration of taxation, public security, municipal construction and public health until 1945 when the Settlement of Kulangsu was recovered by the Kuomintang government. During the period, *By-Laws for the Settlement of Kulangsu, Amoy* was released, in which requirements were stated for the protection of famous rocks on the island, including Seal Rock, Fuding Rock, Flag-Raising Hill Rock, Jimu Rock, Jiguan Rock, Jinguan Rock, Yanwei Rock, Camel Hill Rock, Drum Wave Rock and Sunlight Rock.

◎ 鼓浪石。（朱庆福 摄）
Drum Wave Rock. (Photo by Zhu Qingfu)

浪荡山在英雄山和美华海滩附近，便是工部局时期所称的"骆驼山"，因形似骆驼而得名。因山下有"鼓浪石"，又称"浪洞山"，闽南方言谐音而成"浪荡山"。

升旗山上有1863年厦门海关所建的海关测候所（气象台站）和升旗信号站，引导船只进出厦门港，"升旗山"也因此得名。

英雄山旧称"旗仔尾山"，中华人民共和国成立后为纪念解放厦鼓战役中牺牲的战士与船工改名，现建有英雄园。

鸡母山，则因山顶上巨石像母鸡的头而得名。

◎ 19世纪70年代鼓浪屿升旗山海
关信号站。（白桦 供图）
Customs Signal Station on top
of Flag-Raising Hill in the 1870s.
(Courtesy of Bai Hua)

◎ 燕尾山生态公园。（子健传媒 供图）
Yanwei Hill Ecopark. (Courtesy of Zijian Media)

　　燕尾山上有午炮台，是19世纪后期厦门海关港务管理部门理船厅公署所设，在雾天海上灯塔、航标失灵的情况下指引船只正常行驶。但因为厦门的雾天并不多见，因此海关便以此设施为海关理船厅职员及鼓浪屿岛上居民准确接收和校正钟表时间。海关雇员每周六午间遥望鹭江对岸厦门海关楼顶的大壁钟，到12点整准时鸣炮两响，通知海关及鼓浪屿社区居民准确对时。与此同时，鼓浪屿的天主堂也敲钟12响。这是当时岛上居民校时的一种特殊方式。

　　笔山上有基督徒所称的"祈祷岩"，因19世纪末、20世纪初大英长老会传教士经常率众教徒到这块巨石上祈祷而得名。祈祷岩与日光岩遥遥相对，它是岛上看华美日落的最佳所在。

Langdang (Tidal Wave) Hill sits near Hero Hill and Meihua Beach. It was once called "Camel Hill" during the administration of the Kulangsu Municipal Council after its terrain shaped like a camel's hump. It is now also known as "Langdong Hill" after "Drum Wave Rock" at its foot. Actually "Langdang" is "Langdong" in South Fujian dialect.

On top of Flag-Raising Hill there used to be a meteorological station and a flag signalling station built by Amoy Customs in 1863 to guide ships to and from Amoy Port, which leads to its current name.

Hero Hill, formerly known as "Qiziwei Hill", was renamed in memory of soldiers and boaters who died in the battle of liberating Amoy and Kulangsu in 1949. There is a theme park on the hill in their honour.

Jimu (Hen) Hill is named after a boulder on the top of the hill which looks like a hen's head.

◎ 1924年鼓浪屿燕尾山午炮台。（白桦 供图）
Signal Cannon Emplacement on Yanwei Hill, Kulangsu, in 1924. (Courtesy of Bai Hua)

◎ 笔山公园。（子健传媒 供图）
Bishan Hill Park. (Courtesy of Zijian Media)

On top of Yanwei Hill sits the former site of a Signal Cannon Emplacement built in the late 19th century by the Maritime Affairs Office of Amoy Customs to guide ships on the right navigation course in case the beacon and navigation indicators did not work on foggy days. The facility turned out to be used more often as a signal cannon set to align time for its staff and islanders of Kulangsu as there were few foggy days in Amoy. Every Saturday, employees of Amoy Customs would fire two guns at 12 o'clock as measured by the big clock on the top of the Amoy Customs Tower, across the Lujiang Strait, while the bell in the Catholic Church would also ring at the same time. This was the process of time alignment on the island.

On Bishan Hill there is a large granite slab called Prayer Rock, a name given by Christians because missionaries of the Presbyterian Church of England often took their followers to pray on the granite slab towards the end of the 19th century and the beginning of the 20th century. Facing Sunlight Rock, Prayer Rock is a vantage point to enjoy beautiful sunsets.

鼓浪屿沿岸的海蚀地貌丰富，岩礁峭壁交错，沙滩逶迤，环岛一周，可慢享此种景致：田尾沙滩、大德记沙滩、港仔后沙滩、美华沙滩环绕着小岛，它们有的曾是西人开发的日光浴场和海滨浴场，有的曾经是洋行运送中国劳工出洋的码头。还有三丘田码头遗址，它是鼓浪屿少数尚存的早期码头遗址，是当时鼓浪屿原住民来往厦门与鼓浪屿主要的码头。现存的三丘田码头遗址历经多次修葺，也成为游客上岛的码头之一。

　　鼓浪石仍在，沿着小岛环游，便可遇见它。时光漫漶，石刻与礁石或许比任何记载都留存得更为久长。

◎ 三丘田码头遗址。（子健传媒 供图）
Remains of Sanqiutian Jetty. (Courtesy of Zijian Media)

Kulangsu features rich marine topography along the coast, with rocks, reefs, cliffs and beaches constituting the island's natural landscape. One can admire its beauty by exploring the island. Some of the most impressive sights are the surrounding beaches, such as Tianwei Beach, Dadeji Beach, Gangzihou Beach and Meihua Beach. Some beaches were developed by Westerners for entertainment, whereas others were ports from which foreign firms had Chinese laborers sent abroad to work. Sanqiutian Jetty is one of the few remaining major dock sites from the early developments on Kulangsu. Several repairs and restoration efforts have protected the jetty, which is now one of the docks by which travellers can get to the island.

Strolling around the island, one may see Drum Wave Rock. Time may pass but the cliff inscriptions and reefs will stay much longer, longer than any other records.

◎ 鼓浪屿港仔后海滩。（康伦恩 摄）
Gangzihou Beach of Kulangsu. (Photo by Kang Lun'en)

日光岩和延平文化遗产

在鼓浪屿无惊无扰的渔猎耕种岁月里，明末清初郑成功率领他的军队来到岛上，以此为据守之地，屯营扎寨，操练水兵。在彼时，小岛也曾是郑氏开展海上贸易的基地之一。

追随郑成功的文人雅客也来了。其中，有一个叫"陈士京"的江浙文人，在岛上组织"海外几社"，筑起"鹿石山房"隐居。山房早已不存在，陈士京之墓经过迁移，如今仍在鸡母山的路边，寂寞却也显眼。

郑成功留下了龙头山寨、国姓井，留下了印斗石、拔剑石、覆鼎岩的传说，还留下了厦门最有趣味的中秋博饼习俗，等等。这些和他有关的延平文化遗产，是日光岩下的一段重要历史记忆。1916年，越南华侨黄仲训在日光岩内建造私家别墅时将日光岩区域一并圈入，想建成私家花园。此事引起轩然大波，最后黄仲训迫于压力，不得不将日光岩开放为公园，命名为"鼓浪屿延平公园"。

◎ 日光岩景区。（林乔森 摄）
Sunlight Rock Scenic Spot. (Photo by Lin Qiaosen)

◎ 日光岩景区内的郑成功纪念馆。（康伦恩 摄）

Koxinga Memorial Museum at Sunlight Rock Scenic Spot. (Photo by Kang Lun'en)

Sunlight Rock and Yanping Cultural Relics

The peaceful days of fishing, hunting and farming were no more when Koxinga and his troops garrisoned on Kulangsu during the late Ming and early Qing dynasties. They used the place as a fort to train naval forces, as well as a base for maritime trade.

With Koxinga came his entourage scholars. Among them, a scholar named Chen Shijing from Zhejiang Province organized "Overseas Society" on the island and built "Lushi House" to dwell in seclusion. The house no longer exists and the grave of Chen Shijing was relocated to the roadside of Jimu Hill, isolated, yet conspicuous.

Koxinga is remembered today not only as a national hero but also for his contributions to communities and the many cultural relics he left behind, such as Longtou Fortress, Koxinga's Well, Seal Rock, Sword Rock, Fuding Rock and the most fascinating Moon-cake Gaming custom. Owing to the fact that Koxinga was conferred the title of Yanping County King by Emperor Yongli of the Southern Ming Dynasty, this cultural heritage became relics of a remarkable time in history, all of which was witnessed by Sunlight Rock. In 1916, Huang Zhongxun, a Vietnamese Chinese, bought the site and planned to include the whole scenic area of Sunlight Rock into his private premises as he was constructing his family villa there. This was vehemently rejected by the public and he was eventually forced to open the area to the public and named it "Kulangsu Yanping Park".

◎ 施士洁题写的"古避暑洞"。（康伦恩 摄）

"Ancient Summer Cave" written by Shi Shijie. (Photo by Kang Lun'en)

　　1985年，一座由625块巨型花岗岩雕凿嵌接而成的郑成功雕像在他361周年诞辰时，"站立"在了覆鼎岩上，把剑临风，衣襟飞扬，自此年复一年守望着他曾经护卫的疆土。当年故垒依旧，历史已经经历多少烟云？国姓井里的山泉清冽，是否还能照见几百年的沧海桑田？

　　海拔92.68米的日光岩是鼓浪屿的最高点，亦是鼓浪屿的必游之地。日光岩，别名"晃岩"，位于鼓浪屿龙头山顶，它其实只是一块直径40多米的巨石，而非巍峨的山峦。但站立在它的方寸之地上，凭海临风，极目远眺，天风海涛，鼓岛尽收眼底，风光的确无可比拟。

　　1573年，泉州同知丁一中在日光岩上题了"鼓浪洞天"四个大字。1915年，时任福建巡按使的许世英在这块巨石高处题写"天风海涛"。之后又有近代中国赴美第一人、写有《西海纪游草》的林鍼题的"鹭江第一"，施士洁题写的"古避暑洞"，还有蔡廷锴、蒋鼎文、朱兆莘等的题字。历朝历代的摩崖题刻汇集在日光岩的各处，也成为人文胜景。

In 1985, a huge statue of Koxinga made of 625 pieces of giant granite blocks rose to "stand" on Fuding Rock in celebration of his 361st birthday. Sword in hand and in his armor, the statue watches the territory that Koxinga once defended. The former fort stands intact and the spring water in Koxinga's Well remains crystal clear despite the passage of time.

With an elevation of 92.68 meters, Sunlight Rock is the location of highest elevation on Kulangsu and a must-visit destination for tourists. Also known as "Huangyan Rock", Sunlight Rock is actually a giant rock with a diameter of over 40 meters. Nevertheless, it is ideal for the unrivalled panoramic view of the island between the vast expanse of sea and sky.

Sunlight Rock is also known for its cliff inscriptions by famous people throughout history. It was said that in 1573 Ding Yizhong, then subprefect of Quanzhou, had four Chinese characters "Gu Lang Dong Tian" (Wonderland of Idyllic Beauty) inscribed on Sunlight Rock. In 1915, Xu Shiying, then ombudsman of Fujian, had another inscription of "Tian Feng Hai Tao" (Sky Wind and Sea Waves) on the upper part of the huge rock. Later Lin Zhen, one of the earliest scholars visiting the US in China's modern times as well as the author of *Records on the Travel in the Western Sea*, had his inscriptions "Lu Jiang Di Yi" (Unrivalled Land of Lujiang) carved next to the inscription of "Gu Lang Dong Tian" on Sunlight Rock. There are also "Ancient Summer Cave" by Shi Shijie and other inscriptions by Cai Tingkai, Jiang Dingwen and Zhu Zhaoshen, to mention a few.

◎ 丁一中题写的 "鼓浪洞天"，许世英题写的 "天风海涛" 和林鍼题写的 "鹭江第一"。（康伦恩 摄）
"Gu Lang Dong Tian" (Wonderland of Idyllic Beauty), "Tian Feng Hai Tao" (Sky Wind and Sea Waves) and "Lu Jiang Di Yi" (Unrivalled Land of Lujiang) written respectively by Ding Yizhong, Xu Shiying and Lin Zhen. (Photo by Kang Lun'en)

依着日光岩景区的日光岩寺，俗称"一片瓦"。这座袖珍的寺院实际上是一个天然的石洞，以巨石为顶，再依山形地势而建。日光岩寺是鼓浪屿最早的佛教寺庙，初建时名为"莲花庵"。明朝的比丘尼在巨石下结庵住修，供奉观音菩萨。莲花庵虽然仅有石室一间，明清时期却位居厦门四大名庵之一。明万历十四年（1586）重修，并更名为日光岩寺，此后几经修建，如岩石上的巍巍蜃楼，晨夕之间的梵音钟声如潮涨潮落，与日光岩的天风海涛互为风景，遂成为鼓浪屿最著名的所在。连战的祖父、著有《台湾通史》的连横先生，当年居鼓浪屿时，也留下"日光岩畔钟声急，时有鲸鱼跋浪前"的诗句。

日光岩寺虽小，却不失精巧。1936年，一代高僧弘一法师曾在寺中东厢寮房闭关养静，并为楼房题匾，称"日光别院"，此处如今是弘一大师纪念馆。

◎ 日光岩寺。（陈育萍 摄）
Sunlight Rock Temple. (Photo by Chen Yuping)

◎ 日光岩寺。（陈育萍 摄）

Sunlight Rock Temple. (Photo by Chen Yuping)

Adjacent to Sunlight Rock is Sunlight Rock Temple, commonly known as "One Tile Roof". The tiny temple was actually a natural grotto, with a large rock forming the roof and was built out of the hill. It is the earliest Buddhist temple on Kulangsu and was first named "Lotus Nunnery". In the Ming Dynasty nuns lived and worshipped Guanyin, the Goddess of Mercy, here under the rock that serves as the temple's roof. Although the temple had only a stone hall, it was one of the four most famous nunneries in Amoy during the Ming and Qing dynasties. It was renamed Sunlight Rock Temple when it was renovated in 1586. Afterwards, it underwent several renovations and repairs but managed to survive to become a unique and most famous part of the landscape on Kulangsu. Lien Heng, Lien Chan's grandfather and the author of *The General History of Taiwan*, wrote a poem during his stay on Kulangsu which contains the following lines: "To the ringing of the temple bell by Sunlight Rock, whales sometimes dance between waves."

Small in size, Sunlight Rock Temple was ingeniously designed. In 1936, the eminent Buddhist monk Master Hong Yi spent some time on retreat in the east wing of the temple and inscribed a plaque for where he stayed, "Sunlight Residence". The site is now Memorial of Master Hong Yi.

花间的鼓浪屿，永不归去的春天

榕树的气根守候着岛屿的日升月落。飞来榕在不经意的角落驻足，艳丽的三角梅更是繁花如云。木棉、凤凰花、炮仗花、使君子、曼陀罗、白兰……在属于它们的季节尽情开放，使鼓浪屿的四季从来都不寂寞。草木葳蕤，花开似锦，品种丰富的植物在巷弄里，在庭院中，郁郁葱葱，开得招摇无限。这是鼓浪屿的万国建筑、礁石海浪之外的另一种风景。

亚热带海洋性季风气候的鼓浪屿，阳光充足，海风润泽，降水量丰沛。鼓浪屿不仅是外国人所认为的"尘世的天堂"，亦是植物的乐土。

和外国人因为政治、商旅或者传教而来到异乡一样，和闽南各处的华侨因为落叶归根而聚居鼓浪屿一样，植物们漂洋过海，远渡而来，在鼓浪屿扎根生长。比如岛上随处可见的旅人蕉，早在二十世纪二三十年代就引种栽培于鼓浪屿，为我国最早引种的物种之一。

鼓浪屿的植物经历了两次大的迁徙。第一次是归乡的华侨为了装饰庭院，从海外带回植物；第二次则是1959年华侨亚热带植物引种园成立时，引进了上千种植物资源。

◎ 鼓新路上盛放的三角梅。（杨戈 摄）
Blooming bougainvillea at Guxin Road. (Photo by Yang Ge)

◎ 鼓浪屿上的凤凰花。（童东升 摄）
Flamboyants on Kulangsu. (Photo by Tong Dongsheng)

◎ 木棉花开的春天。（杨戈 摄）
Spring adorned by blooming kapok. (Photo by Yang Ge)

Kulangsu in Flowers and Evergreens

Banyan trees, with their firm air roots deep in the soil, have been growing with the island for centuries. The flying ficus adorns street corners sporadically, accompanied by gorgeous flowers including bougainvillea, kapok, flamboyants, flame vines, the Chinese honeysuckles, thorn apples and white orchids, dressing Kulangsu in a multitude of colors and species during different seasons of the year. Blooming flowers and evergreens are everywhere in back streets and gardens, adding to the beauty of Kulangsu together with the diverse architectures, coastline and spectacular waves.

Endowed with a pleasant sub-tropical marine monsoon climate that is warm and humid, Kulangsu is rich in sunshine with plenty of rainfall. It is a piece of paradise on earth not only in the eyes of foreign residents but also for all flora on the island.

Many plants travelled all the way across the ocean to take roots and grow on Kulangsu together with foreign politicians, merchants and missionaries coming here, as well as with many returned overseas Chinese from all parts of South Fujian who chose to settle down on Kulangsu. One of these plants is the traveller's palm which can be found everywhere on the island. It was introduced and cultivated on Kulangsu as early as the 1920s and 1930s, and is one of the earliest species introduced to China.

Exotic plants on Kulangsu were introduced in large numbers from two sources. The first was with returned overseas Chinese who brought with them many plants to decorate their courtyards and home gardens. The second was in 1959 when the Overseas Chinese Subtropical Plant Introduction Garden was established and thousands of plant species were introduced.

◎ 黄荣远堂别墅里的两棵百岁圆叶蒲葵。（康伦恩 摄）
Two hundred-year-old round-leaf fountain palms in Huang Rongyuan Mansion. (Photo by Kang Lun'en)

　　黄荣远堂别墅前种植的两棵108岁的圆叶蒲葵，是内地最早引种、最高的圆叶蒲葵；还有世界上最高的台湾枣椰（田尾路厦门海关验货员公寓旧址的院内）；曾是国内唯一的一棵柱状南洋杉（毓园林巧稚雕像后）；国内最高、最粗的大叶桃花心木（延平公园国姓井旁）；国内最高的加勒比合欢树、国内最粗的紫檀（华侨亚热带植物引种园内）；胸围直径达153厘米、国内最粗的五棱大戟（内厝澳57号的庭院里），已经158岁了；还有133岁的罗汉松，433岁的古榕树，183岁的杧果树，菽庄花园内的台湾苏铁……植物专家确认拥有189株古树名木的鼓浪屿，位列全国城市建成区中古树名木密度最高。

　　华侨亚热带植物引种园成立于1959年，当时定名为"华侨亚热带植物引种场"，由印尼归侨倡议创办，从海外引进粮油植物良种，通过试验场进行栽培驯化，然后进行推广。引种园因历史原因停办了数年，后来在被誉为新西兰"猕猴桃之父"的园艺学家、鼓浪屿人李来荣等人的努力下复办。引种园曾从五大洲几十个国家引进植物种子资源千余份，得到应用推广的上百种，包括粮食作物、蔬菜、水果、花卉、林木、药材和香料等，在国内率先大量引进香子兰、西番莲（百香果）、剥粒波萝等香饮植物，还有棕榈科、竹芋科、龙舌兰科、天南星科、凤梨科、旅人蕉科等多种室内外观赏植物。

The two 108-year-old round-leaf fountain palms planted in front of Huang Rongyuan Mansion are the earliest and tallest of this species of plant introduced to the Chinese mainland. Other heritage plants include the world's highest date palm from Taiwan (in former Amoy Customs Inspectors' Quarters, Tianwei Road) and many once "the one and only" species in China, such as the columnar araucaria (behind the statue of Lin Qiaozhi in Yuyuan Garden); the largest and thickest mahogany (beside Koxinga's Well in Yanping Park); the highest Caribbean acacia tree and the thickest rosewood (in the Overseas Chinese Subtropical Plant Introduction Garden). There are also the 158-year-old widest royle's spurge with a circumference of 153cm (in the courtyard of 57 Neicuo'ao), the 133-year-old Buddhist pine, the 433-year-old ancient banyan tree, the 183-year-old mango tree and the cycas taiwaniana in Shuzhuang Garden Villa, to mention just a few. Botanists have confirmed that Kulangsu, with 189 heritage trees, boasts the highest density of such trees in urban built-up areas in China.

Originally named "Overseas Chinese Subtropical Plant Introduction Farm", the Overseas Chinese Subtropical Plant Introduction Garden was set up in 1959 by returned overseas Chinese living in Indonesia in an attempt to introduce improved varieties of grain and oil plants from abroad to cultivate and acclimate in the test farm before popularizing them. It was suspended for several years due to historical reasons, but later resumed thanks to the effort of Li Lairong, a native of Kulangsu and an overseas Chinese horticulturalist known as the "father of kiwifruit" in New Zealand. Bringing in more than a thousand species seeds from dozens of countries, of which hundreds were spread beyond the garden, including food crops, vegetables, fruits, flowers, trees, herbs and spices. The garden was often the first in the country to introduce from abroad a large quantity of flavorings and fruits like vanilla, passion fruit and pineapple as well as indoor and outdoor ornamental plants such as palms, arrowroot, century plants, araceae, pineapple and traveller's palm, among others.

◎ 华侨亚热带植物引种园。（康伦恩 摄）
Overseas Chinese Subtropical Plant Introduction Garden. (Photo by Kang Lun'en)

植物是这座岛屿的另一种纪年方式。你看到200岁、300岁甚至400岁的它们，在沉默不语的年轮里，小岛这一两百年的兴与衰恐怕它们最洞若观火。也许从另一个角度来看，植物也是这座岛屿的主人。当那些传教士们或埋骨此地或返回故土，那些南洋华侨的子孙们星散于世界各地，草木们却牢牢扎根，安居岛上。

那也是蔡其矫的诗里所描绘的——

"每一座墙头全覆盖新鲜绿叶，

每一条街道都飘动醉人花香，

蝴蝶和蜜蜂成年不断地奔忙，

花间的鼓浪屿，永不归去的春天。"

Plants are another way to read the history of Kulangsu. At the age of 200, 300 and even 400, they have witnessed in silence the great changes of the island over the past centuries. In a sense,

these plants are also hosts of the island. While those missionaries were either buried here or back home, and later generations of people of Chinese descent from Southeast Asia may now reside all over the world, the plants and trees have been taking roots on the island, firmly and securely.

These were vividly depicted by Cai Qijiao, a well-known Fujian poet, in one of his poems:

"Green vines and foliage spread on every wall,

Sweet flower fragrance wafts down every street.

Butterflies and bees are busy all year round,

And this is Kulangsu, in flowers and evergreens."

◎ 巷弄里冬日盛放的炮仗花。（康伦恩 摄）
Flame vines blooming in winter. (Photo by Kang Lun'en)

◎ 凤凰花盛开在鼓浪屿的巷弄里。（童东升 摄）
Blooming flamboyants in back streets. (Photo by Tong Dongsheng)

文化交融——公共地界与国际社区

　　1920年，一个名叫保罗·哈钦森的美国人在记述鼓浪屿时写道："这是一个令人惊奇的小岛，在如此狭小的岛屿上，居然拥有如此之多风格迥异的建筑，如此之多的英才与风云人物。可以说，无论是在艺术、教育，还是医学、建筑，鼓浪屿都扮演了一个时代先锋的角色，遥遥领先中国其他地方，如果不算加利福尼亚的帕萨迪纳，鼓浪屿上的富人比地球上任何地方都多。"

　　纵观鼓浪屿的历史，这一座位于出海口的原本毫不起眼的小岛，因为历史的原因，随着1843年厦门的开埠、1903年鼓浪屿公共地界的确立以及随后华侨归国定居的热潮，在中西文化的合力之下，蜕变成一个世所瞩目的岛屿。

Cultural Integration: Public Land and International Settlement

It is said that in 1920, an American named Paul Hutchinson said of Kulangsu: "It is an amazing island, with so many buildings in a diverse range of styles and so many people of brilliance and talent. It can be said that Kulangsu is far ahead of other parts of China and paves the way in art, education, medicine and architecture. Actually, Kulangsu boasts more rich people than any other places on Earth, excluding Pasadena of California."

A review of the history of Kulangsu reveals that it used to be a tiny unassuming island sitting at the estuary of the sea. For historical reasons, Amoy was opened as one of the treaty ports in 1843 and in 1903, the International Settlement of Kulangsu was established, followed by an upsurge of overseas Chinese returning to China and settling down on Kulangsu. As a result of the joint influence of Chinese and Western cultures, the island began to draw worldwide attention.

◎ 鹭江两岸。（林乔森 摄）
Kulangsu and Amoy across the Lujiang Strait. (Photo by Lin Qiaosen)

◎ 俯瞰鼓浪屿。（林乔森 摄）
Bird's eye view of Kulangsu. (Photo by Lin Qiaosen)

　　鼓浪屿岛民、著名作家舒婷在她写鼓浪屿的著作《真水无香》里，这样描写自1843年后的百年鼓浪屿："反思小岛100年来，那些现代社区管理（工部局、会审公堂）、现代通信（大北电报公司）、现代海关税收（理船厅公所、吡吐庐）、现代贸易（德记洋行）、现代教育（养元、福民小学，寻源、毓德、怀德、英华中学）、现代医疗（博爱医院、救世医院）、宗教传播（福音堂、三一堂、天主堂）……在弹丸之地上四处盛开，就会深感经由中西文化激剧碰撞、顺应，从缓慢的农耕节奏中，一下子就弹奏成'人杰地灵'的韵律。"

　　比如基督教入闽第一人、美国归正教牧师雅裨理懂得中文，他曾经在东南亚闽南籍华侨居住地学会了闽南话，所以当1844年1月，时任清朝福建布政使的徐继畬在厦门兼办通商事务，会晤英国第一任驻厦门领事记里布时，雅裨理便担任他们的翻译。他还向徐继畬讲述了世界各国的历史地理概况。这些后来都被徐继畬写进了《瀛寰志略》一书中，这本书对中国的戊戌变法和日本的明治维新都产生了积极的影响。而在19世纪中叶，徐继畬及其著作是西方人特别是传教士们观察中国的风向标。《瀛寰志略》不仅是中国人观察世界之窗，也是西方人探寻中国文化的一条路径。

In her book *Away from the Hubbub,* Shu Ting, a famous female writer and resident of Kulangsu, comments on the island since 1843: "We could have a chance to reflect on what has happened on the island over the past hundred years. The modern community management (Kulangsu Municipal Council and Kulangsu Mixed Court); modern communications network (the Great Northern Telegraph Company); modern customs taxation (Maritime Affairs Office and Residence of Amoy Customs Deputy Commissioner); modern trade (Tait); modern education [Yangyuan and Fumin primary schools, and Xunyuan, Loktek, Huaide and Anglo-Chinese (Yinghua) high schools]; modern medicine (Pok Oi Hospital, Hope Hospital); religious influences (Gospel Hall, Trinity Church, Catholic Church)…, all these things emerged in the small island as a result of the meeting and compromise between Chinese and Western cultures which transformed the slow-paced island into a dynamic, progressive space for outstanding people to excel."

David Abeel, a missionary of the American Reformed Church, was the first evangelist who came to Fujian. He spoke Chinese and learnt South Fujian vernacular from South Fujian overseas Chinese living in Southeast Asia. In January 1844, he was appointed as the interpreter at a trade talk between the Fujian deputy governor Xu Jiyu and the first British Consul in Amoy Henry Gribble. Abeel introduced Xu into the history and geography of countries around the world. These were later recorded in a book written by Xu which was entitled *Short Records of the World* (*Yinghuan Zhilue*). The book had exerted a positive impact on China's Reform Movement in 1898 and Meiji Restoration in Japan. Its influence went far beyond just Asia. In the mid-19th century, Xu Jiyu and his works were a standard by which Westerners, particularly missionaries, could learn about China. In this sense the book was not only a window for Chinese people to see the outside world, but also an avenue for Westerners to explore Chinese culture.

在日光岩上留有题刻"鹭江第一"的福建闽侯人林鍼，幼年移居厦门，在已经成为五个通商口岸之一的城市里，在洋商、水手、传教士中学会了英文，以在洋行担任翻译和教授中文为生。1847年春天，林鍼受美国花旗银行聘请，前往美国教习中文。两年后，他返回厦门，定居鼓浪屿，将他在美国的游历和见闻写成《西海纪游草》一书，此书成为近代第一部中国人亲历海外生活的文字记录。

　　中国拼音文字运动的先驱卢戆章也葬在这里。受到传教士所创的闽南白话字的启发，卢戆章于1892年写成了厦门话的切音字专著《一目了然初阶》一书。书中拟订了他称为"中国第一快切音新字"的拼音方案，提出了"语言一律"的思想。为了纪念他，他所葬的墓园旁去往海边的小路，如今被修成"拼音路"，石头小路上镌刻着汉语拼音字母。

　　一百多年的风云激荡，因为华洋共管的历史，鼓浪屿在当时的中国是一个自由先进的小岛，环境宜居，文化开放。鼓浪屿，因此成为中国东南沿海一颗熠熠生辉的明珠。中西文化的交融和碰撞，不仅使得鼓浪屿成为领先同时代其他地域的国际社区，也使得鼓浪屿人开眼看世界，获得更从容与广博的视野。

◎ 拼音小路上的卢戆章头像。
（子健传媒 供图）
Statue of Lu Zhuangzhang on Pinyin
Road. (Courtesy of Zijian Media)

Another story is about Lin Zhen, who had his inscription "Lu Jiang Di Yi" (Unrivalled Land of Lujiang) carved on Sunlight Rock. From Minhou, Fujian, Lin Zhen came to live in Amoy, one of the five opening treaty port cities, when he was a child and learnt to speak English from foreign businessmen, sailors and missionaries, which enabled him to secure a job as a translator and Chinese language teacher in a foreign firm. In 1847, he went to the United States to teach Chinese at the invitation of Citibank. Two years later, he returned to Amoy and settled down on Kulangsu where he wrote and published the book *Records on the Travel in the Western Sea*, which is the first written account in modern times of a Chinese travelling to the West.

We also have the story of Lu Zhuangzhang, initiator of the Chinese Pinyin language movement who was buried on Kulangsu. Inspired by South Fujian POJ invented by foreign missionaries, Lu wrote a monograph on the Xiamen vernacular entitled *Chinese Alphabets: A Primer* in 1892. In the book, he proposed a Pinyin system which he called "An Easy New Alphabetic Chinese Language", and put forward the idea of "language uniformity". To remember him, the path leading to the sea beside the cemetery where he was buried is now named "Pinyin Road", and is inscribed with Chinese Pinyin.

This special history of joint management by Chinese and Westerners turned Kulangsu into a small, well developed island with a more open culture than other places in China at the time. Kulangsu has since become a shining pearl along southeast China coast. The blending and collision of Chinese and Western cultures have not only made Kulangsu an international settlement leading China's other regions throughout history, but allowed its people to view the world with a more open mind.

◎ 鼓浪屿街头旧貌。（陈亚元 供图）
Street scenes of Kulangsu in the old days. (Courtesy of Chen Yayuan)

◎ 旧时鼓浪屿上的取水设施。（陈亚元 供图）
Well water drawing on Kulangsu in the old days. (Courtesy of Chen Yayuan)

一个让异乡人愉悦的岛屿

1911年11月8日，美国归正教会牧师、鼓浪屿寻源书院主理毕腓力在他的《厦门纵横——一个中国首批开埠城市的史事》的序言中，写下了这样一段话——

"也许沿着这个蜿蜒伸展的海岸，没有同样的小岛曾有过比它更引人兴趣的故事。它仅有八英里宽，许多轰动的事件在此地与毗邻发生。数百年来，它是凶狠的海盗与野蛮的冒险家的相聚之地……它是一个经历无数次残酷斗争的剧场及战略要地。或者说它是通往所有受满洲人、长毛反叛者、荷兰人及日本人觊觎的辽阔领土（包括台湾）的大门。"

鸦片战争前，鼓浪屿人烟稀少，偏安一隅，行政上为归属于厦门市镇所设四社中的和凤前后社辖下的五保之一，即"鼓浪屿保"，涉外事务则由设在厦门的兴泉永道署管理。但正如毕腓力所言，"厦门是中国的一个贸易中心，有着无比优越的港口，很早以前就为西方的旅行者和商人所熟悉"。

A Most Welcoming Island

On November 8, 1911, Philip Wilson Pitcher, a missionary of the American Reformed Church and headmaster of Xunyuan Academy on Kulangsu, wrote in the preface of his book *In and About Amoy: Some Historical and Other Facts Connected with One of the First Open Ports in China*:

"No other place along this winding stretch of coastline has probably ever had more interesting and exciting stories than the island. It is only eight miles wide, yet many sensational events have taken place here and around its neighboring areas. For centuries, it has been where fierce pirates and brutal adventurers met... It is a strategic location that has hosted numerous vicious battles. We may say it is the gateway to all the vast territories (including Taiwan) coveted by Manchurians, barbarians, the Dutch and the Japanese."

Kulangsu was sparsely populated and isolated before the Opium War. It used to be "Kulangsu Neighborhood", one of the five neighborhoods under the administration of Hefeng Qianhou, one of the four communes in Amoy, and its foreign affairs were handled by the commissioner of Xinghua-Quanzhou-Yongchun Administration based in Amoy. The island attracted attention to itself as Amoy became one of China's first five treaty ports during the war, but others have recognized its potential before, and as Pitcher puts it: "Amoy as a trading centre in China is endowed with incomparably superior harbors and ports, and was known to Western travelers and traders long ago."

◎ 鼓浪屿南部一角。（陈亚元 供图）
The south beach of Kulangsu. (Courtesy of Chen Yayuan)

◎ 和记洋行仓库遗址。（子健传媒 供图）
Former site of Warehouse of Boyd & Co. (Courtesy of Zijian Media)

◎ 鼓浪屿上的英国领事馆。（陈亚元 供图）
The British Consulate on Kulangsu. (Courtesy of Chen Yayuan)

　　1845年，一位叫德滴的苏格兰籍商人在厦门开设德记洋行后，和记、宝记、旗昌、美时、瑞记等洋行相继开办，洋行的经营地点在厦门，会所和住宅则设在鼓浪屿。

　　在三丘田码头附近，留有当年的和记洋行仓库的遗址。和记洋行成立于19世纪50年代末，最初经营船舶维修业务。该处遗址仅存花岗岩条石砌成的外墙残余，以及石砌门窗的边框。

　　1863年，英国在鼓浪屿的领事馆落成，英国领事也正式从厦门搬到鼓浪屿办公。也是在这一年，由英国人控制的海关税务司署在厦门设立，它的职员宿舍和许多附属机构如海关税务司公馆、海关副税务司公馆、理船厅公所等都设立在鼓浪屿。西班牙、法国、美国、德国、日本等国的领事馆也相继在鼓浪屿落成。

　　自此，外国人逐渐居留鼓浪屿，还有教堂、教会学校、医院和邮局等密集开办，各国风格的洋楼别墅在岛上风景优美的空旷之地建起。到1890年，鼓浪屿上已经有外国居民300余人。

In 1845, a Scottish merchant named James Tait set up Tait & Co. in Amoy. Other foreign firms were established afterwards, such as Boyd & Co., Pasedag & Co., Russell & Co., Milisch & Co. and Lessler & Co. They operated in Amoy but had their private clubs and residences on Kulangsu.

Near the Sanqiutian Jetty exists the former site of the warehouse of Boyd & Co. Started up in the late 1850s, Boyd & Co. was originally in the ship maintenance and repair business. Now, the site has only the remains of the exterior wall of granite strips and frames of stone windows and doors.

In 1863, construction of the British Consulate on Kulangsu was completed, and the British Consul moved his office from Amoy to Kulangsu. In the same year, the British-controlled Customs Taxation Administration was set up in Amoy with its staff quarters and many subsidiary organizations built on Kulangsu, such as Customs Taxation Officers' Quarters, Residence of the Amoy Customs Deputy Commissioner, and the Maritime Affairs Office. Consulates of Spain, France, the United States, Germany, Japan and other countries were also established on the island.

Since then, more and more foreigners have settled down on Kulangsu, bringing churches, missionary schools, hospitals and post offices. Various styles of villas and mansions were built on the beautiful island. By 1890, Kulangsu had more than 300 foreign residents.

◎ 鼓浪屿上的美国领事馆。（陈亚元 供图）
The US Consulate on Kulangsu. (Courtesy of Chen Yayuan)

来到鼓浪屿的外国人非常注重道路等公共设施的建设。1878年，鼓浪屿成立了"道路墓地基金委员会"，由驻鼓浪屿的领事、海关官员、传教士、商人等组成每年选举一次的委员会。该委员会的筹款方式是征收人头税、人力车辆税、马匹税、其他车辆税、坟地税等各种税款，然后利用所征税款在鼓浪屿修建街道，整治水沟，栽种树木等。

1900年，厦门洋务分局奉福建巡抚之命，在鼓浪屿设置巡捕局，地址在兴贤宫。巡捕长最初由英籍人士担任，巡捕为印度锡克教徒，后来又增加了巴基斯坦伊斯兰教徒，还有中国山东籍、台湾籍巡捕及日籍巡捕。

这些举措让19世纪末20世纪初的鼓浪屿面貌一新："这里平展的道路已经修成，并有人专管，以期保持道路的良好状况"，"沿着路旁栽种了树木……使这里带有一种森林的气息"。居住岛上的外国人也不断增加，洋人的住宅遍布岛上。在居留异乡的外国人眼中，风景优美的鼓浪屿已经"像欧洲南部的城市一样"呈现"一幅悦人心目的图画"。这一切与对岸那个尚未开始公共建设、街道狭窄肮脏的厦门城，简直有天壤之别。

◎ 二十世纪初的鹭江两岸。（陈亚元 供图）
Kulangsu and Amoy across the Lujiang Strait at the beginning of the 20th century. (Courtesy of Chen Yayuan)

◎ 鼓浪屿巡捕局巡捕合影。（白桦 供图）
The Kulangsu Municipal Police. (Courtesy of Bai Hua)

Foreign settlers on Kulangsu paid great attention to the construction of roads and other infrastructure. In 1878, the "Kulangsu Road & Cemetery Fund Committee" was set up, composed of foreign consuls, customs officers, missionaries and businessmen on Kulangsu, and the members were annually elected. The committee collected various taxes, such as poll taxes, motor vehicle taxes, horse drawn carriage taxes, cemetery taxes and other taxes, which were used to build streets, clean the island and plant trees.

In 1900, as directed by the Fujian governor, the Amoy Foreign Affairs Administration established a police station based in Xingxian Temple of Kulangsu, which was originally staffed with Indian Sikhs, under the guidance of a British chief. Later on, more people were employed, including Pakistani Muslims, Chinese from Shandong and Taiwan as well as Japanese.

These initiatives had given Kulangsu a new look in the late 19th and early 20th centuries: "There were smooth roads built and maintained to keep them in good condition". "Trees were planted along the roadsides... to give it a forest-like atmosphere". The number of foreign settlers was also increasing, with their houses becoming a common sight on the island. In the eyes of these immigrants, the scenic Kulangsu was "like a city in Southern Europe", presenting "a most picturesque scene". All this was a sharp contrast with Amoy on the other side of the Lujiang Strait, where construction of public infrastructure had not started yet and the streets were narrow and dirty.

◎ 鼓浪屿万国俱乐部。（陈亚元 供图）
Amoy Union Club, Kulangsu. (Courtesy of Chen Yayuan)

　　翟理斯在《鼓浪屿简史》里写道："当时的外国人可以去俱乐部阅读书报，打保龄球、台球和网球，在剧院观看精彩的演出，海边每年举办一次为期两天的赛马会，可以在活动场公开举行草地网球赛，也可以在那些拥有适用草地的有钱人的公馆里私下举行。可以在美丽的沙滩上散步聊天，黄昏去海里游泳，还能准时在餐桌上看到厦门的报纸。""环绕着鼓浪屿散步即使有些单调，但还是舒心的。""除此之外，鼓浪屿还有物价低廉和商品多样化的市场，有益健康的气候以及周围美丽的风光，并且有直达电报通往全球大多数的地方，'鼓浪洞天，鹭江第一'，的确名不虚传。"

　　在翟理斯的笔下，鼓浪屿是个"特别让异乡人愉悦的岛屿"。

In *A Short History of Koolangsu*, Herbert Allen Giles wrote: "At that time, foreigners could join clubs for reading, bowling, billiards and tennis; or go to theatres for entertaining performances. A two-day horse race was held by the seaside annually, and there were lawn tennis matches held openly in public spaces, or in private mansions of the rich with befitting lawns. One could take a walk along the beautiful beach, or go swimming in the sea late in the afternoon before coming back home to the dinner table, and for some reading of the Amoy newspaper which arrived in due time." "Walking around the island of Kulangsu was enjoyable even if a little boring." "In addition, Kulangsu was known for its gentle climate and beautiful scenery, markets offering a rich variety of commodities at very good prices, and it was a place where direct telegraphs could be sent to most parts of the world. It was indeed a 'Wonderland of Idyllic Beauty' and an 'Unrivalled Land of Lujiang'".

From these descriptions by Giles, we can see Kulangsu was a "most welcoming island" indeed.

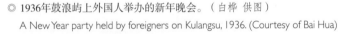

◎ 1936年鼓浪屿上外国人举办的新年晚会。（白桦 供图）
A New Year party held by foreigners on Kulangsu, 1936. (Courtesy of Bai Hua)

◎ 熙熙攘攘的鼓浪屿旧时街景。（白桦 供图）

Busy street of Kulangsu in the old days. (Courtesy of Bai Hua)

公共地界的社区建设与管理

为了消除日本人对鼓浪屿的垂涎，1902年1月10日，中外代表在日本驻厦门领事馆签署了《厦门鼓浪屿公共地界章程》。1902年11月21日，光绪皇帝批准鼓浪屿正式成为公共地界，这是中国近代史上唯一一个清廷主动开放的公共地界，是继上海后的中国第二个公共地界，而且是十三个西方列强共管的最后一个公共地界。

根据《厦门鼓浪屿公共地界章程》，鼓浪屿作为一个公共地界，土地属中国皇帝，管理权经清政府授权，由工部局的常年公会、特会、界内工部总局、会审公堂共同掌管。

Community Building and Management of the International Settlement

To better safeguard Kulangsu from Japanese invasion, representatives of China and foreign countries signed *Land Regulations for the Settlement of Kulangsu, Amoy,* at the Japanese Consulate in Amoy on January 10, 1902. On November 21st of the same year, Emperor Guangxu approved Kulangsu to be an international settlement, the first time in China's modern history, for the country to take initiative and open itself to the outer world. It was the second international settlement in China after Shanghai and the last one co-administered by 13 Western powers.

As stipulated in the *Land Regulations for the Settlement of Kulangsu, Amoy*, the land of Kulangsu as a piece of public land shall belong to the Chinese emperor and the right of management shall be authorized by the Qing Government to be jointly held by the Annual Conference of the Municipal Council, Special Conference, the General Municipal Council of the Settlement and Mixed Court.

◎ 20世纪20年代的鼓浪屿。（白桦 供图）
Kulangsu in the 1920s. (Courtesy of Bai Hua)

1903年1月，鼓浪屿公共地界工部局成立。鼓浪屿工部局在岛上至少有过三处办公地点。现存遗址即为最早租用的洋行建筑遗址，位于鼓新路与三明路交叉处（鼓新路40号）。这座殖民地外廊建筑的主体已于2007年倒塌，但仍保留了一些残券砖壁。

　　初期的工部局局董由洋人纳税者会（洋人纳税者会指的是每年1月召开的由有存案的财产在1,000银圆以上、每年纳税5银圆以上的鼓浪屿外国居民参加的常年公会，俗称"洋人纳税者会"。公会会议上，公举工部局董事，审查工部局工作及财政状况。）公举6人（工部局的洋人局董需有存案的财产在5,000银圆以上，或每年纳租捐500银圆以上，同一洋行、同一教会、同一公司或同居一屋的，只允许派1人作为候选人），另由兴泉永道举荐居住鼓浪屿的殷实华侨乡绅一人充任华董。出身台湾首富家族、内渡鼓浪屿的林尔嘉就曾任华董14年之久。

◎ 1910年鼓浪屿工部局巡捕监视犯人劳动。（白桦 供图）
Prisoners laboring under the surveillance of a Kulangsu Municipal policeman, 1910. (Courtesy of Bai Hua)

◎ 鼓浪屿工部局收据。（白桦 供图）

Receipt from the Kulangsu Municipal Council. (Courtesy of Bai Hua)

In January 1903, the Kulangsu Municipal Council was established. Its office was relocated at least three times. The existing site, at the intersection of Guxin Road and Sanming Road (40 Guxin Road), was its earliest office, a building constructed by foreign enterprise in Veranda Colonial Style, which the Council rented. The building collapsed in 2007, but some of its brick wall is still there.

In its early stages, the directors of the Council board were composed of six people elected by the Kulangsu Foreign Taxpayer Society. The organization refers to the annual conference of foreign residents on Kulangsu whose registered property was worth at least 1,000 silver dollars and whose annual tax payment was more than 5 silver dollars. At the conference, the elected director of the Municipal Council was to review the performance and financial condition of the Council. The foreign directors of the Municipal Council had to be those who had a registered property of over 5,000 silver dollars, or an annual donation of more than 500 silver dollars. Only one person was allowed to be appointed as the candidate from the same foreign firm, church, company or household. The Chinese director, who had to be a well-off returned overseas Chinese on Kulangsu, was recommended by the Xinghua-Quanzhou-Yongchun Administration. One of them was Lin Erjia (Lim Nee Kar), who was born to Taiwan's richest family and came to settle down on Kulangsu. He was appointed and acted as a Chinese director for 14 years.

工部局设有巡捕房，官员、差役由兴泉永道及福建洋务总局委派。后巡捕队因扩大，分为内勤和外勤两部分。内勤分书记处（下设会计、出纳各1人）、警务处（管理巡捕队及侦探队）。此外，还分设财政股（主办征收地租、牌照税和罚款等）、建设股（设有筑路队负责修建路面、水沟以及植树等）、卫生股（设有清道队和清洁队，负责界内卫生工作）。

The Kulangsu Municipal Council had a police station under its jurisdiction, with officers appointed by the Xinghua-Quanzhou-Yongchun Administration and the Fujian General Foreign Affairs Administration. With the increase of staff members, the police station was divided into two departments, handling the internal and external affairs separately. The former was subdivided into sub-secretariat (with one accountant and one cashier) and police administration (in charge of policemen and detectives). The latter was divided into finance administration (responsible for the collection of rent, license tax and fines), construction administration (in charge of the construction and repair of roads and ditches as well as tree planting) and public health administration (with teams responsible for road sweeping and cleaning within the settlement territory).

◎ 鼓浪屿工部局遗址。（子健传媒 供图）
　Remains of the Kulangsu Municipal Council. (Courtesy of Zijian Media)

China
4
Land regulations
1926

LAND REGULATIONS FOR THE SETTLEMENT OF KULANGSU, AMOY.

Preamble. Whereas China establishes Kulangsu as a Settlement, in order that due provision may be made for constructing roads and jetties, and keeping them, and existing roads and jetties in repair, for cleansing, lighting watering and draining the Settlement, establishing and maintaining a Police force thereon, making Sanitary Regulations, paying the wages and salaries of persons employed in any Municipal Office or capacity and for raising the necessary funds for any of the purposes aforesaid, the following regulations are hereby drafted and submitted to the Chinese Foreign Office for discussion with the Foreign Ministers and subsequent confirmation ~~by Imperial Rescript~~.

Limits of the Settlement. 1.—The limits of the Settlement wherein these Regulations shall be binding are an imaginary line drawn at 100 feet outside low water mark round the Island of Kulangsu, lying W. S. W. of the Island of Amoy and having roughly speaking an area of a little over 1½ square miles.

Annual General Meetings. 2 — It being necessary and expedient that provision be made for the appointment of a Municipal Council for the management of Municipal matters, the Senior Consul for the time being shall, in the month of January in each year, call a general meeting of voters, ~~to attend which the Taotai shall depute a Chinese gentleman of good standing, who shall afterwards be~~

17 se 75

◎ 鼓浪屿工部局发行的邮票。（白桦 供图）
A stamp issued by the Kulangsu Municipal Council. (Courtesy of Bai Hua)

工部局拟定了《鼓浪屿工部局律例》管理鼓浪屿，其中许多条例涉及日常生活，规范岛民的种种行为，连对家畜的畜养也有详细的讲究。如今看来，像是岛民的行为准则，十分有趣，但也使得鼓浪屿成为一个文明有序的岛屿，比如：

"游澡

凡有在海边行状令人可厌者，准巡捕立即拘拿。游澡者必须穿游澡衣袂，欲换之时，不准在海边。

脚踏车

不准乘脚踏车于人烟稠密之处，以致伤害行人，违者拿办不贷。

家畜

鼓浪屿公界内，凡有畜养鸡、猪、牛及一切家畜等类，理宜约束，不宜放在路上肆行，因有违碍本局章程，除出示禁后，倘有不遵示禁，仍将此等家畜放出肆行糟蹋公路，一经本局巡捕触见，即将此等畜类充公，并饬传畜养主人到会审公堂理罚不贷。

残酷家畜

凡本界内居民，如有殴打或残酷家畜等者，必须拘捕究办。

割伐树木

凡逾越花园以及在公路割伐树木者，因有逾过私界及在公路割伐树木之情由数件，而且常在花园墙界内等寻拾柴火者并割伐树木者，损坏甚多，各巡捕等有受严命，倘有故违者，定即拘拿究办不贷。

养犬执照

本公界内所有畜狗之家，须于每年正月间到本局领给牌照，若无领牌之狗，肆行公路，一经巡捕触见，立即击毙。

纸炮

本公界内不准居民于夜间十一点至晨七点以内燃放爆竹及种种花炮。"

The Kulangsu Municipal Council had worked out *Regulations for the Management of Kulangsu*, many of which involved social etiquettes for islanders in their daily life, including detailed restrictions concerning keeping and raising livestock. The rules and regulations functioned like today's codes of conduct for the islanders which made Kulangsu a clean and well-managed place. The following were some of the regulations:

Swimming

Anyone who does not behave decently on the beach shall be arrested immediately. Swimmers shall wear their bathing suit or trunks, and shall not change them on the beach.

Pedal Cycling

Do not ride a pedal cycle in crowded places to avoid injury to pedestrians. Offenders shall be punished.

Livestock

All livestock such as chickens, pigs and cattle shall be restrained and are not left unattended on the road within the territory of Kulangsu settlement. This prohibition from the Municipal Council shall be abided by, otherwise the livestock shall be confiscated and their owners be summoned to court for penalty.

Brutalizing Livestock

Persons within the settlement who beat or brutalize domestic animals must be arrested.

Unauthorized Tree Cutting

Those who trespass private gardens to collect firewood or cut down trees in the garden or on the road shall be severely punished since several such cases have occurred recently. Any violation of this law shall be punished by the police.

Dog Raising License

All dog raising households within the settlement are required to obtain a license from the Municipal Council in the first lunar month each year. Any unlicensed dogs found running about on the road shall be shot immediately by the police.

Firecrackers & Fireworks

Residents are not allowed to set off firecrackers and other kinds of fireworks between 11:00 p.m. and 7:00 a.m.

鼓浪屿工部局设立时还参照上海工部局的方式，成立了鼓浪屿会审公堂（现笔山路1号），裁决中外纠纷案件，行使公共地界的司法权。会审公堂主要审议鼓浪屿公共地界内涉及中国人的诉讼案件，如涉及外国人，则须与外国领事会同审理。鼓浪屿会审公堂不仅审理案件、化解纠纷，还更多地开展了一些社会治理的工作，比如审理一些擅取花木、倒卖坟山等跟社会管理、市政文明有关的案件。

◎ 会审公堂审理的情景。（陈亚元 供图）
A sitting of the Mixed Court. (Courtesy of Chen Yayuan)

Upon the establishment of the Kulangsu Municipal Council, a Mixed Court (now at 1 Bishan Road) to judge disputes and exercise judicial power of the international concession was set up, following the practice of the Shanghai Municipal Council. The Mixed Court mainly deliberated Chinese lawsuits within the settlement of Kulangsu and the judgment was to be jointly made by the court and the foreign consul if foreigners were involved. The court also participated in social governance by handling cases concerning public welfare and municipal administration, such as taking away landscaping without authorization and speculative reselling of cemetery space.

◎ 会审公堂。（康伦恩 摄）
The Mixed Court. (Photo by Kang Lun'en)

◎ 1927年法国领事馆职员家属与中国保姆。（白桦 供图）
Families of the staff working in the French Consulate and the Chinese nannies, 1927. (Courtesy of Bai Hua)

　　《厦门鼓浪屿公共地界章程》规定：鼓浪屿公共地界"内有应添筑修理新旧码头、道路、设立路灯，蓄水通沟，设立巡捕，创立卫生章程，酌给公局延请办事上下各项员役及设法抽取款项，作为以上所用各项之公费"。依靠着工部局这样一个颇为现代化的管理机构，鼓浪屿的社区建设和治理在当时的中国颇为先进，比如修筑海堤；对岛上道路的修建、维护和保养；铺设水泥排水管，治理污水；在岛上建起公共厕所和设置垃圾箱；制定了死亡登记规则和筑墓许可制度；成立为社区服务的家庭访问护士队伍等。

　　到19世纪末，鼓浪屿主要道路的结构体系已经形成：北面有笔架山环线道路；南面则是日光岩、岩仔脚环线道路；东南面是鹿耳礁环线道路；在岛的东部和南部，由环线道路延伸出若干海滨放射道路。

　　另外还有《鼓浪屿外人租借地律例》对岛上环境保洁、环境保护、墓葬等做了规定。鼓浪屿的整体环境再次得到提升，居住在岛上的外国人真心喜爱和赞赏这个岛屿。毕腓力在1910年出版的《厦门纵横——一个中国首批开埠城市的史事》一书中写道："鼓浪屿，这座不规则的椭圆形小岛，长约1英里，宽约0.5英里，与厦门片帆可至。由于它优越的地理环境以及迷人的自然风光，再加上优美的港口和群山的怀抱，沿着整个中国海岸再找不到比这里更美的地方。因此，鼓浪屿成了商人和传教士群体在远东地区的居住地。"

　　毕腓力还在他的另一本著作《在厦门五十年：厦门传教史》里写道："'鼓浪洞天'的意思是：鼓浪屿是天堂之下最令人快乐的地方。"

◎ 鼓浪屿工部局旧大楼。（白桦 供图）
Former building of the Kulangsu Municipal Council. (Courtesy of Bai Hua)

As stipulated in the *Land Regulations for the Settlement of Kulangsu, Amoy,* "There are old and new wharfs and roads to be built and repaired, street lamps to be installed as well as water storage and ditch cleaning projects to be completed. In addition, a police station is to be set up and sanitary regulations are to be formulated and released. Therefore the Municipal Council should provide staffing and funding to handle all these expenses." Thanks to a modern management agency like the Municipal Council, Kulangsu was able to pave the way in China with regards to community development and governance, such as seawall construction, maintenance of roads on the island, sewage treatment, public toilets building and the placement of bins for public use. They also oversaw the implementation of a death registry and tomb building permission system, as well as a team of nurses to serve the community, visiting home if necessary.

By the end of the 19th century, a network of main roads on Kulangsu was taking shape, with Bijia Hill Loop Road running to the north, Sunlight Rock and Yanzijiao Loop Road to the south, Lu'erjiao Loop Road to the southeast, and further roads to the south and east coast extended from the main loop roads.

There was also *Regulations for Kulangsu Foreign Settlement* which made stipulations for the cleaning and protection of the environment, as well as for the management of cemeteries. Kulangsu was made more beautiful and greatly admired by foreign settlers. Philip Wilson Pitcher wrote in his book *In and About Amoy: Some Historical and Other Facts Connected with One of the First Open Ports in China:* "Kulangsu, an irregularly oblong island about one mile long and half a mile wide, is only a narrow stretch of water away from Amoy. No other place along the China coastline is better than this island, boasting great atmosphere and beautiful landscape with ports and mountains. That is why Kulangsu became a settlement in the Far East for merchants and missionaries."

He voiced similar admiration in *Fifty Years in Amoy: Or, a History of the Amoy Mission, China*, another book of his: "'Gu Lang Dong Tian' (Wonderland of Idyllic Beauty) actually means that Kulangsu is the most pleasant place beneath heaven."

归侨参与国际社区建设与完善

19世纪末，台湾被日本占领，有许多台湾富商内渡鼓浪屿，这其中有台湾两大家族，板桥林家和雾峰林家。前一个家族有修建菽庄花园的林尔嘉和修建八卦楼的林鹤寿，后一个家族有孙中山的密友、献身革命、在岛上建有宫保第的林祖密将军。

1920年至1930年，早年下南洋发家致富的闽南移民纷纷入住鼓浪屿。这是因为鼓浪屿的居住环境宜人，教育以及文化氛围优良，而他们的家乡泉州、漳州一带尚处于动乱之中，土匪恶霸层出不穷。鼓浪屿与其生活习俗相近，语言相通，加上有公共租界的安全护佑，工部局现代化的社区管理，南洋华侨纷纷在鼓浪屿这个宜居之地修建华屋，安家置业。岛上华人人口快速增长，远远超过外国人的数量。曾有统计，鼓浪屿上的华侨侨眷，占岛上人口近一半之多。台湾首富家族的林尔嘉、印尼糖王黄奕住、越南富商黄仲训、菲律宾木材大王李清泉、橡胶大王林文庆以及黄秀烺、许经权等，都在鼓浪屿上置地兴业。

◎ 越南许姓华侨所建的亦足山庄。（林乔森 摄）
Yizu (Contentment) Villa, built by a Xu Family, who returned from Vietnam. (Photo by Lin Qiaosen)

◎ 出身台湾雾峰林家的林祖密将军的宫保第。（康伦恩 摄）

House of General Lin Zumi from the well-known Lin Family in Wufong, Taiwan. (Photo by Kang Lun'en)

Contributions of Returned Overseas Chinese: Design and Improvement of the International Settlement

At the end of the 19th century, Taiwan was occupied by Japanese invaders. Many business people there moved to the mainland and settled down on Kulangsu. Among them were two Lin families from Banchiau and Wufong. Well known in Taiwan at the time, the Lin family from Banchiau is remembered today for Lin Erjia (Lim Nee Kar) and Lin Heshou, who had Shuzhuang Garden Villa and Bagua Mansion (Eight Trigrams Mansion) built respectively; while the Lin family from Wufong is renowned for one of its family members, General Lin Zumi. A close friend of Sun Yat-sen, Lin devoted himself to revolution and had an official mansion on the island.

Between 1920 and 1930, immigrants from South Fujian who had moved to Southeast Asian countries and made a fortune there returned to settle down on Kulangsu owing to the island's pleasant living environment, excellent education and cultural atmosphere; while their hometown in Quanzhou or Zhangzhou was still in turmoil, with rampant bandits and other threats. The pleasant day to day life, language spoken, security guarantee in the international settlement and the modern community management by the Municipal Council attracted many overseas Chinese to choose Kulangsu as a place to build their mansions and villas. The population of Chinese on the island was growing rapidly, far outnumbering foreign settlers. Statistics showed that families of overseas Chinese living on Kulangsu accounted for nearly half of the island's population, and many purchased land and built houses there, including Lin Erjia from Taiwan's richest family, Oei Tjoe (Huang Yizhu), a sugar tycoon in Indonesia, Huang Zhongxun, a wealthy man from Vietnam, Li Qingquan, a timber magnate in the Philippines, Lim Boon Keng, a rubber mogul, Huang Xiulang and Xu Jingquan, among others.

华侨们汲取了西方现代文明，引入先进技术，将鼓浪屿社区公共基础设施的营造和提升作为推动社会革新的工具，投资商业的同时亦积极参与鼓浪屿的各种建设和治理，成为鼓浪屿管理的坚实力量，比如华董在工部局董事会中的名额从原先的1人最多曾争取到1929年的5人，获得了更大的发言权。鼓浪屿上也成立了不少华人自己的团体组织，比如"华人纳税者会""华民公会""华人议事会"等，从而使得鼓浪屿进入一个新的黄金时代。

正因为华侨投入巨资参与鼓浪屿的建设与开发，电话通信、电灯电力、自来水设施等市政基础设施在这一个时期兴建，鼓浪屿居民的生活更加现代便捷，生活品质得以进一步提升。

◎ 旧时鼓浪屿上的自来水滤水池。（陈亚元 供图）
Tap water filter tank on Kulangsu in the old days. (Courtesy of Chen Yayuan)

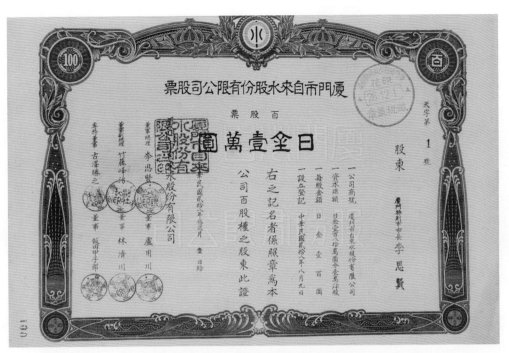

◎ 1939年厦门市自来水公司股票。（白桦 供图）

Stock of Amoy Water Supply Company, 1939. (Courtesy of Bai Hua)

These returned overseas Chinese drew on modern Western civilization, bringing back to Kulangsu advanced construction technology and improvements to public infrastructure. They invested in businesses while at the same time, actively participated in various building and management affairs of the island to become a staunch force in the governance of Kulangsu. The number of Chinese directors on the board of the Municipal Council increased from an initial one to five in 1929, resulting in a large influence over the decision making process concerning issues on Kulangsu. Many Chinese organizations were established, such as the Chinese Taxpayers' Society, Chinese Association and Chinese Council, which ushered in a new period of prosperity for Kulangsu.

It was with the participation of overseas Chinese in the development and management of the international settlement, particularly with their large investment in construction of infrastructure, such as telecommunications, electricity and water supply facilities, that people on the island began to improve their living standards.

◎ 厦门自来水公司旧址。（林乔森 摄）

Former site of Amoy Water Supply Company. (Photo by Lin Qiaosen)

　　在自来水引入鼓浪屿之前，鼓浪屿居民或饮用井水，或购买通过渡船运送到鼓浪屿的"船仔水"。1917年，为改善城市生活品质和饮水卫生条件，黄秀烺、黄奕住、林振勋等众多华侨富商共同筹设了厦门自来水公司。1921年，厦门自来水公司委托林振勋之子、海归工程师林全诚担任总工程师，聘请美国工程师勘测水源、选址、测量和设计，选用德国西门子公司设备，最终建成中国东南沿海最早投入使用的自来水供水系统，特别是过滤池与臭氧处理技术在远东地区无可匹敌，居当时世界先进水平，甚至被称为"远东第一水厂"。

　　1929年，鼓浪屿工部局因岛上两万居民饮水和火警消防之需，商请厦门自来水公司在鼓浪屿设立公共供水设施，服务于岛上居民。1930年林全诚及俄籍工程师在厦门与鼓浪屿设计建设上下水码头，在鼓浪屿码头附近建两座低位水池，在日光岩山麓及鸡冠山建高位水池，铺设输水管道，并在鸡冠山建设备用房和管理人员用房（现漳州路24号的鼓浪屿自来水供水设施旧址）。1932年，厦门自来水公司开始向鼓浪屿岛上居民供应自来水，备运水船4艘、拖船1艘，每天从厦门将滤清的水运到鼓浪屿西仔码头，用电机将水抽入水池，再通过管道输水到全岛各处。

Before tap water was introduced to Kulangsu, residents of the island drank water from wells, or bought "boat water" shipped by ferry. In 1917, Huang Xiulang, Oei Tjoe, Lin Zhenxun and other rich overseas Chinese businessmen joined hands to collect funds and set up the Amoy Water Supply Company. In 1921, they entrusted a returned overseas Chinese engineer Lin Quancheng, son of Lin Zhenxun, as the chief engineer and brought in American engineers for surveys, location selection, measurement and design. Finally, they adopted equipment made by Siemens and completed the installation of the tap water supply system. This was the earliest such system put into operation in Southeast China coastal areas. The state-of-the-art filter tank and ozone treatment technologies, advanced by international standard at the time, were second to none in the Far East.

In 1929, the Kulangsu Municipal Council requested the Amoy Water Supply Company to build public water supply facilities on Kulangsu to address the needs of its 20,000 residents for supply of drinking water and water for fire control. 1930 saw many construction projects completed, designed and built by Lin Quancheng and his Russian engineer colleague, including water supply and sewer jetties in Amoy and Kulangsu. They also constructed water storage areas near the Kulangsu Dock and in the foothills of Sunlight Rock and Jiguan Hill, with an equipment room and a room for managerial staff in Jiguan Hill (now former site of Kulangsu Water Supply Facilities at 24 Zhangzhou Road), together with the necessary water pipes. In 1932, residents on the island were able to use tap water. Four water carriers and a tugboat were provided to deliver filtered water to Xizi Dock of Kulangsu every day. Water was pumped into the storage units by electric motors and conveyed to every household on Kulangsu through pipes.

◎ 厦门自来水公司旧址。（林乔森 摄）
Former site of Amoy Water Supply Company. (Photo by Lin Qiaosen)

1871年，丹麦大北电报公司在鼓浪屿率先实现电报通信。1904年，电话技术首先由日本人引进厦门和鼓浪屿。1908年，林尔嘉创办了厦门最早的电话公司——厦门德律风公司。同时，日本人在鼓浪屿开设了川北电话公司。当时这两家电话公司设备比较落后，没有海底电缆，厦鼓两地无法跨海通话。黄奕住先后收购上述两家公司后，在鼓浪屿设"商办厦门电话股份有限公司"鼓浪屿接线站（现龙头路102号）。随后，黄奕住购置美国开洛公司共电式交换机、电话机等设备，聘请上海的钱咸昌为总工程师，于1923年铺设厦鼓海底电缆，架设电杆线路。1924年，厦鼓实现通话，安装电话达到600门之多。随后，电话覆盖区域扩展至漳州等地。1935年，厦门海关的无线电通信设施竣工，鼓浪屿实现了无线电通信。

◎ 厦门海关通讯塔旧址。（子健传媒 供图）
Former Amoy Customs Communications Tower. (Courtesy of Zijian Media)

◎ 鼓浪屿电话公司旧址。（康伦恩 摄）
Former Kulangsu Telephone Company. (Photo by Kang Lun'en)

In 1871, Great Northern Telegraph Company (Denmark) started operation of sending and receiving telegrams on Kulangsu. In 1904, the telephone was introduced to Amoy and Kulangsu by the Japanese. In 1908, the first local telephone company Amoy Telephone Company was established by Chinese businessman Lin Erjia (Lim Nee Kar) and Kitagawa Telephone Company was set up by the Japanese on Kulangsu a few years later. At that time the equipment of the two companies was lagging behind elsewhere without submarine cables, meaning cross-strait calls between Amoy and Kulangsu were not available. Later, Oei Tjoe acquired the two companies and set up a Kulangsu exchange station named Commercial Amoy Telephone Limited (now at 102 Longtou Road). He also purchased equipment including common battery switchboards and telephone sets from American Kellogg Switchboard and Supply Co. and brought in Qian Xianchang from Shanghai as the chief engineer to set up submarine cables, telephone poles and lines in 1923. In 1924, the first phone call between Amoy and Kulangsu was made, followed by the installation of 600 sets of telephone, and the extension of service to Zhangzhou and other areas over time. In 1935, construction of radio communications facilities of Amoy Customs was completed to make radio communications available on Kulangsu.

1928年至1934年间，缅甸华侨王紫如、王其华兄弟借鉴马来西亚槟城菜市场的经营经验，与工部局订立契约，在鼓浪屿上修建了"鼓浪屿市场"（现海坛路15号）。这也是华侨兴建的岛上唯一具有公益性质的商业与文化娱乐综合设施。市场有20多个店铺、几十个摊位，场地宽敞，通风良好，给排水设施完备，摊位按商品种类设置，荤素干湿分区出售，是当时闽南地区最现代化的菜市场。接着，王氏兄弟又在市场楼上修建了一座戏院兼电影院——延平戏院。延平戏院建筑面积2,700多平方米，戏院内设楼座和池座，约600个座位，可以演戏、说书和放电影。延平戏院是鼓浪屿第一座现代电影院，以放映外国影片为主，市场东门外还有讲古场。鼓浪屿最具市井生活气息的区域得以修建完成，至今这一带也仍是鼓浪屿的商业中心。

　　鼓浪屿工部局甚至在1935年的年度报告中大为称赞这个市场给鼓浪屿的市场带来的改进："因有公共市场之设备，故一切鱼肉蔬菜杂肆尽移入其中，而龙头中街大多数店屋得乘机改建或翻新，而呈新款之气象焉。""本岛公共市场之卫生状态，确有保持其满意之程度，故无论顾客方面或公众健康上大体整洁上，均认其为一大恩物焉。"

◎ 延平戏院旧址。（康伦恩 摄）
Former Yanping Theatre. (Photo by Kang Lun'en)

◎ 鼓浪屿市场旧址。（康伦恩 摄）
Former Kulangsu Market. (Photo by Kang Lun'en)

Between 1928 and 1934, Wang Ziru and Wang Qihua, two brothers of returned overseas Chinese from Burma, signed a contract with the Kulangsu Municipal Council and set up Kulangsu Market (now at 15 Haitan Road) based on their experience in running a food market on Penang Island in Malaysia. It was the only commercial, cultural and recreational complex with public welfare ever built by overseas Chinese on Kulangsu, with more than 20 shops and dozens of stalls. The complex was spacious, with high quility ventilation systems, as well as complete water supply and drainage facilities. Stalls were organized by types and categories, and meat and vegetables, as well as wet and dry goods, were sold in separate sections. It was, at the time, the most modern market in South Fujian.

After that, an attached theatre was built upstairs with the name "Yanping Theatre" by the brothers. Covering a floor space of more than 2,700m^2 with balconies and stalls, the theatre had a capacity of some 600 seats and was used for theatrical performances, storytelling and films. It could be called the first modern theatre on Kulangsu, and most films shown were of foreign origin. Outside the east gate of the market was a site for storytelling. With the completion of the complex, the most urban section of Kulangsu began to develop, and the district is still the commercial center of Kulangsu today.

The Kulangsu Municipal Council spoke highly in its 1935 annual report of the improvement of the local environment brought about by the market:

"Thanks to the well-equipped facilities provided in the public market, all food and stalls were able to move in and most storefronts along the street had to rebuild or renovate themselves to take on a new look." "The sanitary condition of the public market has been satisfactory, which is a blessing to both the customers and the public health."

华侨掀起的房地产开发与商业浪潮

华侨富商还在鼓浪屿和厦门掀起了房地产开发的热潮，也开启了厦门的新城市建设。

主导厦门新城建设运动的林尔嘉，随父林维源内渡鼓浪屿，他出身台湾首富家族——板桥林家，是公共地界时期鼓浪屿的华商领袖。林尔嘉不仅曾任厦门保商局总办兼厦门商务总会总理、农工商部顾问、民国初年的参议院候补委员和福建省行政讨论会会长等职，还曾出任鼓浪屿公共地界工部局董事会华人董事长达14年。

1918年，在越南经营房地产开发的南安籍华侨巨商黄仲训创办黄荣远堂，开始在鼓浪屿开发房地产。他投资十万银圆修建了黄家渡码头，在鼓浪屿建起了五六十座别墅。印尼侨领黄奕住开办黄聚德堂房地产公司，在小小的鼓浪屿上建起一百六十多座别墅，建筑面积达41,457.7平方米，居地产投资的首位。黄奕住还在鼓浪屿兴建了第一条带骑楼的商业街——日兴街（今龙头路）。后来，骑楼街道推广至厦门的旧城改造，成为留存至今、颇具特色的厦门装饰风格街区。

◎ 鼓浪屿第一条带骑楼的商业街（今龙头路）。（康伦恩 摄）
The first commercial street lined with arcade buildings on Kulangsu, now Longtou Road. (Photo by Kang Lun'en)

Real Estate Development and Commercial Activity Facilitated by Overseas Chinese

Rich overseas Chinese helped boost the local economy by developing real estate on Kulangsu and in Amoy, which ushered in a period of new city development.

Lin Erjia (Lim Nee Kar) was a pioneer in this new Amoy building campaign. Born to once the richest family in Banchiau, Taiwan, he moved to Kulangsu with his father Lin Weiyuan. During the period when Kulangsu was an international settlement, Lin Erjia was a leader of Chinese businessmen, appointed as the president of the General Office of Amoy Bureau of Commerce and Amoy Chamber of Commerce as well as advisor to the Department of Agriculture, Industry and Commerce. He was also elected in 1912 as an alternate member of the senate of the Republic of China and president of the Fujian Administrative Consultative Conference. He acted as the Chinese director of the Board of the Municipal Council of Kulangsu for 14 consecutive years.

In 1918, Vietnamese Chinese Huang Zhongxun, with ancestry from Nan'an, Quanzhou, established his real estate development company "Huang Rongyuan Mansion" and began to develop real estate on Kulangsu. He invested 100,000 silver dollars (or about 10 million *yuan* today) in the construction of Huang's Ferry Pier and built over fifty villas. Another returned overseas Chinese Oei Tjoe from Indonesia set up his real estate company "Huang Jude Villa" and was the biggest property investor on the island, constructing over 160 buildings with a total floor space of 41,457.7m². He also developed Rixing Street (now Longtou Road), the first commercial street lined with arcade buildings on Kulangsu. Later on, this style of street design was further adopted in the renovation of old sections of Amoy to become modern city blocks of the distinctive Amoy Deco Style.

◎ 林尔嘉与外国客人合影。
（白桦 供图）
Lin Erjia (Lim Nee Kar) having a photo taken with his foreign guests. (Courtesy of Bai Hua)

◎ 菲律宾木材大王李清泉。（白桦 供图）
Li Qingquan, a timber magnate in the Philippines. (Courtesy of Bai Hua)

在印尼经营糖业的郭春秧来到鼓浪屿之后，在鼓浪屿闹市中心区锦祥街道两旁独资兴建成片的楼房，并在港仔后建洋楼、别墅多处。菲律宾的木材大王李清泉和叔父投资成立了"李岷兴公司"，他们除了在鼓浪屿修建自住的别墅"容谷"和"李家庄"，还在厦门的中山路、中华路、大同路等地建造了数十幢商住两用楼。仅在中山路海口，李清泉自己便建造了11幢楼房。

这是鼓浪屿房地产与建筑业特别繁荣的时代。从1949年的厦门营造厂登记表来看，当时鼓浪屿上从事建筑业的有不少商户：有许春草创办于1918年8月的信合营造厂、坤泰营造厂、振兴营造厂、建成营造厂等；还有建筑材料厂，比如1919年，印尼华侨陈森炎先生集资14万银圆，在鼓浪屿康泰路12号创办了南洲有限公司花砖厂，并于1921年投产。

Another returned overseas Chinese Guo Chunyang, a tycoon in Indonesia's sugar industry, invested in the development of buildings along Jinxiang Street in the downtown area of Kulangsu together with villas and mansions around Gangzihou Beach. Li Qingquan, a timber magnate in the Philippines, made a joint venture with his uncle to set up "Li Minxing Company". In addition to their family villas such as "Banyan Valley Villa" and "Li Family Villa", they constructed dozens of mixed residential and commercial buildings on Zhongshan Road, Zhonghua Road, and Datong Road in Amoy. On Haikou Section of Zhongshan Road alone, Li Qingquan constructed 11 such buildings.

That was a period when real estate development and construction industries boomed on Kulangsu. According to the registration of Amoy construction companies in 1949, many businesses were engaged in the construction industry on Kulangsu at the time. Among them were Xinhe Construction, Kuntai Construction, Zhenxing Construction and Jiancheng Construction, founded by Xu Chuncao in August 1918. There were also factories producing building materials. For instance, Chen Senyan, an Indonesian overseas Chinese, raised 140,000 silver dollars (or some 14 million *yuan* today) in 1919 to set up Nanzhou Tiles Co., Ltd at 12 Kangtai Road, Kulangsu, which was put into operation in 1921.

◎ 李家庄。（子健传媒 供图）
Li Family Villa. (Courtesy of Zijian Media)

地产业繁荣的同时，鼓浪屿的近代银行业也随之崛起。1921年，黄奕住联合有银行管理经验且在政界颇具人脉的胡笔江、《申报》社长史量才等人，在上海成立中南银行。"中南"二字的意思是中国与南洋汇通联络。1922年，中南银行在厦门设分行，并在鼓浪屿设立办事处（现龙头路100号）。中南银行的股东们都是商家巨擘，在南京、武汉、香港等地开设分行。中南银行还曾是中国的发钞银行，1927年发行额达1,700万元（占全国十分之一），最高发行额曾达到7,000万元，而且到1935年停止发行为止，从未发生过信用问题。它是近代海外华侨回国投资创办的最大的银行，也是华侨投资创办的最大企业。

在黄奕住的支持下，1920年李清泉创办了菲律宾第一家华侨私人商业银行"中兴银行"，后发展成为菲律宾最有影响的银行。1925年，中兴银行在厦门设立它在中国的第一家分行。

华侨们一腔热血，希望实业兴国。他们创办各类企业，比如最早在鼓浪屿创办的淘化大同便是当时民族工业的代表，该公司所出品的酱油、酱菜也是老厦门人味觉记忆的一部分。李清泉、黄奕住、黄秀烺等还曾经联手，希望以建设漳龙路矿为重点，开发闽南和福建，奈何时局混乱，他们壮志未酬，徒留遗憾。

◎ 鼓浪屿中南银行旧址。（康伦恩 摄）
Former China & South Sea Bank, Kulangsu. (Photo by Kang Lun'en)

Keeping abreast with the boom of the real estate industry, Kulangsu's modern banking industry also experienced rapid growth. In 1921, Oei Tjoe joined hands with well-known banker Hu Bijiang who had vast management experience in banking and strong connections in political circles, and Shi Liangcai, President of *Shun Pao* (*Shanghai News*) to establish the China & South Sea Bank Limited. The name "China & South Sea" itself implied a connection between China and Southeast Asia. In 1922, the bank branched out in Amoy and set up an office in Kulangsu (now at 100 Longtou Road). The bank also had branches in Nanjing, Wuhan and Hong Kong with big merchants as shareholders. The China & South Sea Bank Limited was also once one of China's banks of circulation, issuing 17 million *yuan* in 1927 (accounting for one-tenth of the country's total), with the highest circulation of 70 million *yuan*. By the time it stopped note issuance in 1935, it had never experienced credit problems. It was the largest bank and company invested and founded by overseas Chinese in modern China.

With the support of Oei Tjoe, Li Qingquan founded China Bank, the first private commercial bank run by overseas Chinese in the Philippines, in 1920, which later became one of the most influential banks in the Philippines. China Bank opened its first branch in Amoy, China in 1925.

Aiming high and in the hopes of making their motherland prosperous, many overseas Chinese set up all kinds of enterprises, such as Amoy Food Limited. first set up on Kulangsu, which was a representative of the national industry at the time. The soy sauce and pickles produced by the company are still part of the memory of older generations in Xiamen today. Li Qingquan, Oei Tjoe and Huang Xiulang had even planned to join hands to develop South Fujian and Fujian in general by constructing Zhangzhou-Longyan Railway, only to find that they could not accomplish this ambitious plan in the chaotic social conditions of the time.

◎ 淘化有限公司商标。（陈亚元 供图）
Trademark of the Amoy Tinning Co. Ltd.
(Courtesy of Chen Yayuan)

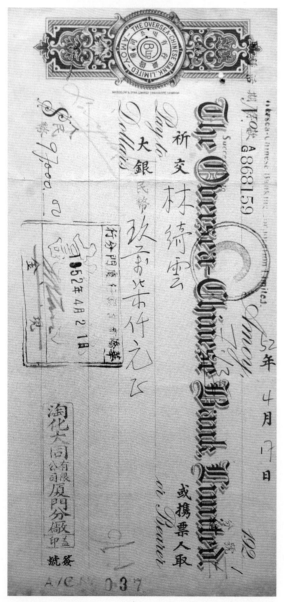

◎ 华侨银行汇票。（陈亚元 供图）
A bill of exchange drawn under The Oversea-Chinese Bank
Limited. (Courtesy of Chen Yayuan)

近现代华侨对厦门的投资在国内城市中排名前列，他们的前瞻足以光照一个时代。故人音尘不绝，华侨富绅们的传奇早已被一座岛屿深深铭记——

出洋谋生、以剃头挖耳起家成为巨富的黄奕住，拒绝改变国籍，将南洋的妻子和儿女留在当地，忍受着"一家之团聚而不可得，无限痛苦"的悲伤，携巨资回到鼓浪屿。他不仅在鼓浪屿建起了"中国第一别墅"——黄家花园，更在母亲74岁生日那天，请来戏班子，大宴宾朋。当日，黄奕住让人在黄家花园前放了一个大木桶，内装满染有红色颜料的银圆。愿意拿的，每人可以拿一个。拿了的，手指也染红了，一时洗不掉，便不能再拿。贺寿的，看寿星的，看戏的，拿银圆的，人潮从厦门渡海涌到鼓浪屿，黄家花园一时人山人海……在那二三十年间，闽南流传着一句话"要想富，就学黄奕住"。

又因为他幼年失学，因此乐于捐资助学：不仅以母亲的私名"慈勤"在岛上创办女学，还捐助了厦门大学、北京大学、复旦大学、暨南大学、南开大学、岭南大学、上海商科大学等。他的小女儿黄萱，既接受现代教育，也接受了良好的闺阁教育，古文造诣很深，后来成为国学大师陈寅恪晚年的助手，二人共同工作了13年，她协助陈寅恪完成的著作，累计超过百万字。

◎ 曾被誉为"中国第一别墅"的黄家花园。（康伦恩 摄）
Huang Family Villa was once reputed as "The Best Villa in China". (Photo by Kang Lun'en)

Overseas Chinese had made greater investments in Amoy than in any other city at home in China's modern times. Their forward-looking approach had resulted in great successes and they are remembered now for their contributions.

Seeking his fortune abroad and starting as a barber and ear cleaner, Oei Tjoe refused to change his nationality after he made a big fortune. Bearing the pain of leaving his wife and children as well as the comfort of home in Indonesia, he returned to Kulangsu with huge sums of money and built Huang Family Villa, known at the time as "The Best Villa in China". It is said that Oei Tjoe was a filial and generous son who celebrated his mother's 74th birthday by inviting an opera troupe to give performances and entertaining his guests with lavish feasts. An anecdote about the event was that Oei Tjoe had a big barrel filled with silver dollars dyed red placed in front of the villa that day. Whoever liked could take one. Those who took the dollar would have their fingers dyed red and would not take more since the red dye did not easily wash away. It was said that the event had attracted so many people and there was an endless flow of visitors to the Huang family from Amoy to Kulangsu by ferry. During a period of 20 to 30 years when Oei Tjoe was at his prime time, there was even a saying going round South Fujian, "Learn from Oei Tjoe if you want to be rich".

Oei Tjoe is also remembered for his generous donation to education because of his own lack of school education. He not only established a women's school on the island after his mother's name "Ciqin", but also made donations to Amoy University, Peking University, Fudan University, Jinan University, Nankai University, Lingnan University and Shanghai College of Commerce, among others. His youngest daughter Huang Xuan received both modern education and traditional Chinese education for women, accomplished in ancient Chinese. She later became the assistant to Chen Yinke, a master of Chinese culture, in his later years and worked together with him for 13 years to have written books totaling over one million characters.

◎ 黄家花园建筑细部。（康伦恩 摄）
Part of Huang Family Villa. (Photo by Kang Lun'en)

还有新加坡华侨林文庆，曾在新加坡开设过第一家中国人办的西药房九思堂，做过孙中山的机要秘书兼医官，于1912年任职南京临时政府卫生部总监，1916年出任外交部顾问……他在马六甲首次引种橡胶成功，被誉为"橡胶之父"；他与黄奕住等合资创建了"和丰银行""华侨银行""华侨保险公司"，成为新马华人金融业的先驱。林文庆18岁就获得英国女皇奖学金，成为获该项奖学金的第一个华人。他曾为厦大鞠躬尽瘁。自1921年接受陈嘉庚邀请出任厦门大学校长，一直到1937年厦门大学改为国立他才辞职回新加坡。他和他的第二任妻子、殷承宗的姑姑殷碧霞（厦门第一位执教的女性）在笔山上的居所宴客酬宾。

这些故人故事，不仅被史志记录，鼓浪屿的流岚与落日、海风与潮汐，一定都记得。

◎ 林文庆。（白桦 供图）
Lim Boon Keng. (Courtesy of Bai Hua)

◎ 鼓浪屿林文庆故居。（蔡松荣 摄）
Former residence of Lim Boon Keng, Kulangsu. (Photo by Cai Songrong)

Another well-remembered overseas Chinese was Lim Boon Keng (Lin Wenqing) of Singapore, who was a physician, government official, entrepreneur and diplomat. He set up Jiusitang Western Pharmacy, the first such establishment run by Chinese in Singapore and served as a confidential secretary and medical officer for Sun Yat-sen. He also served as Inspector General of the Ministry of Health of the provisional government of Nanking in 1912 and as an adviser to the Ministry of Foreign Affairs in 1916. He was the first to introduce rubber to Malacca and was known as the "Father of Rubber". He joined investment with Oei Tjoe and established "Ho Hong Bank", "The Oversea-Chinese Bank Limited" and "Oversea-Chinese Insurance Company" to become a pioneer of Chinese financial industry in Singapore and Malaysia. At the age of 18, Lim became the first Chinese to win a Queen's Scholarship. He had worked hard for Amoy University as its President at the invitation of Tan Kah-kee in 1921 until 1937 when he resigned and returned to Singapore as the university changed into a national university. He and his second wife Grace Yin, the well-known pianist Yin Chengzong's aunt (the first woman teacher in Amoy), often treated their friends to dinner or coffee at their residence in Bishan Hill.

All these stories and people have become legends that perpetuate themselves generation to generation.

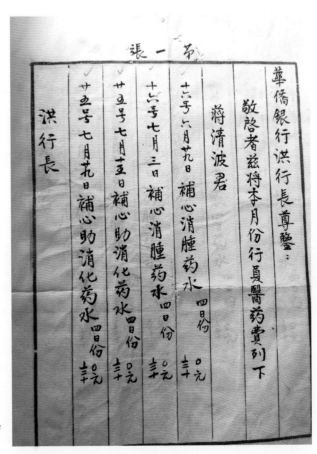

◎ 华侨银行来往信函。（陈亚元 供图）
Correspondence between The Oversea-Chinese Bank Limited. (Courtesy of Chen Yayuan)

万国建筑———一席流动的盛宴

俄罗斯作家果戈理说过，建筑是世界的年鉴，当歌曲和传说都缄默的时候，只有它还在说话。

华美堂皇、形态各异的万国建筑无疑是鼓浪屿最闻名、最令人惊叹的符号。

完好地保留着中外各种建筑风格之建筑的鼓浪屿，有"万国建筑博览园"之誉。岛上现存的900余栋历史风貌建筑，除了作为世界文化遗产的主要元素，还拥有以下保护标签：

2005年，美国领事馆旧址、日本领事馆旧址、汇丰银行公馆旧址、天主堂、三一堂、安献堂、八卦楼、西林·瞰青别墅、亦足山庄、菽庄花园10处13座"鼓浪屿近代建筑"，被福建省人民政府公布为第六批省级文物保护单位。

2006年，"鼓浪屿近代建筑"被国务院公布为第六批全国重点文物保护单位。

2017年11月，"鼓浪屿近现代建筑群"入选"第二批中国20世纪建筑遗产名录"。

◎ 鼓浪屿万国建筑博览园。（朱庆福 摄）
The world's architecture on Kulangsu. (Photo by Zhu Qingfu)

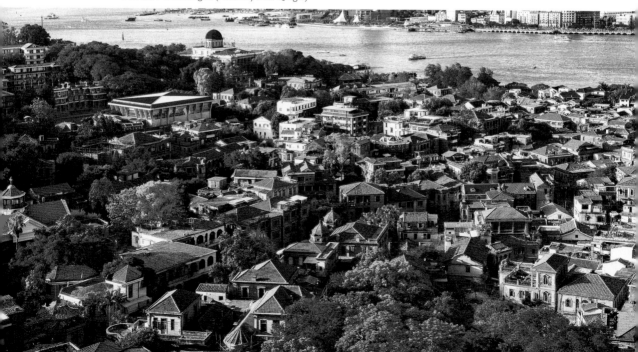

◎ 鼓浪屿英雄山上的建筑。（康伦恩 摄）
Buildings on Hero Hill, Kulangsu. (Photo by Kang Lun'en)

Rich Diversity of Architectural Styles: A Feast for the Eyes

Russian writer Nikolai Gogol once wrote: "Architecture is also a chronicle of the world: it speaks when both songs and traditions are silent." Kulangsu is an excellent example of this idea, and its buildings tell of its rich history.

There are so many architectural masterpieces in both Chinese and Western styles here, which are kept intact and earn Kulangsu the moniker of "An Exhibition of the World's Architecture". Over 900 such buildings surviving today are a major factor of Kulangsu's status as a world cultural heritage site and many are under protection by Chinese governments at state and provincial levels.

In 2005, "Collection of Modern Buildings of Kulangsu" consisting of 13 buildings at 10 sites was listed as historical sites under protection by the Fujian Provincial Government, including the Former US Consulate, Former Japanese Consulate, Former Residence of HSBC's President, Catholic Church, Trinity Church, Anxian Hall (Seventh Day Adventist Church), Bagua Mansion (Eight Trigrams Mansion), Xilin & Kanqing Villas, Yizu (Contentment) Villa and Shuzhuang (Bean Plantation) Garden Villa.

In 2006, these buildings were inscribed on the list of major historical sites under the state protection by China State Council.

In 2007, "Collection of Modern and Contemporary Buildings of Kulangsu" was listed as one of the "20th-Century Architectural Heritage Masterpieces in China".

在19世纪中叶到20世纪中叶的百年间，鼓浪屿是东亚和东南亚区域独具特色的对外交流窗口。闽南传统风格、殖民地外廊式、西方古典复兴式、现代主义风格、装饰艺术风格等建筑风格汇聚于一座小岛，并在多元文化交流的土壤中生发出具有本土建筑特征的"厦门装饰风格"，影响辐射到沿海其他区域。

建筑是物化的历史记忆，它直观直接，而且毫无隐瞒地告诉你时间所有的来与去。当穿行在静谧小巷中的阔大庭院，老屋门窗柱栏上的花卉雕刻，卵石铺就的园中小径，华丽讲究的地板、家具，漂洋过海而来的异域植物，都是无法隐藏的曾经繁华印记。也许还能遇见深深宅院里的传奇过往。那是历史的余温，是家族的血脉，如岛上的古榕树一般盘根错节，与这座岛屿的过去及现在紧密相连。

Kulangsu was once a unique gateway to the outside world, where exchanges between the East Asia and Southeast Asia took place within the span of a hundred years from the mid-19th to mid-20th centuries. The place is itself an amalgamation of Eastern and Western architectural styles, including the traditional South Fujian Style, Veranda Colonial Style, Western Classical Revival Style, Modernist Style, Art Deco Style and other styles. It is from this coexistence of diverse cultures that the distinctive local "Amoy Deco Style" developed and grew, which has now spread along the coastline.

Architecture is a physical imprint of history, which tells, without deceit, stories of the past. Pay a visit to old mansions in quiet back streets and you would be impressed by their spacious courtyards and gardens, the floral carvings on their columns, beams, doors and windows, the garden paths paved with cobbles, the gorgeous and exquisite floors and furniture, and the exotic plants from across the sea. All these are the visible remnants of past prosperity that are still there and visible. You may also learn about the urban legends that have developed around these big houses. They are the blood, sweat and tears of families, as intertwined with the island as the ancient banyan trees, closely linked to its past and present.

◎ 俯瞰菽庄花园。（康伦恩 摄）
Bird's eye view of Shuzhuang Garden Villa. (Photo by Kang Lun'en)

◎ 天主堂钟楼。（康伦恩 摄）

The bell tower of the Catholic Church. (Photo by Kang Lun'en)

◎ 四落大厝与周围建筑相映成趣。（杨戈 摄）

Four–Compound Mansion and its surrounding buildings stand side by side. (Photo by Yang Ge)

最闽南的传统红砖民居

　　闽南话把房子称作"厝"。闽南红砖古厝主要分布于厦、漳、泉等地。闽南红砖古厝，红砖红瓦，外在建筑艳丽，而内在朴实端庄。闽南红砖古厝吸收了中国传统文化、闽越文化和海洋文化的精华，成为闽南文化的重要组成部分。

　　"有庭院深深的大夫第和四落大厝。铜门环凹凸剥蚀，击一声绵长，再击一声悠远，声声清亮如磬。红砖铺砌的天井里，桂香一树，兰花数盆，月季三两朵。檐前滴水青石，长年累月，几被岁月滴穿。中堂的长轴山水，檀香案上的青瓷描金古瓶，甚至洒扫庭院的布衣老人的肩头，似蒙着薄薄一层百年的浮尘。"

South Fujian Style Traditional Red-Brick Dwellings

In South Fujian dialect, houses are called *cuo*. South Fujian red brick ancient houses are mainly in Xiamen, Zhangzhou and Quanzhou of South Fujian. These houses with their red bricks and tiles look gorgeous but are elegantly simple inside. Drawing on the best of traditional Chinese culture, Minyue Culture and Maritime Culture, they constitute an important part of South Fujian Culture.

"I am always deeply impressed by the serene courtyard of the former official residence Dafudi Mansion, and the well-known ancient Four-Compound Mansion. The copper door bells, though weathered and covered with rust, still ring far and wide with a sound as clear as a bell can be. There are sweet scented osmanthus, orchids and Chinese roses in the red brick paved courtyard, and the drainage slabs in front of the eaves are almost worn away by exposure to the weather, generation after generation. The long landscape scroll painting adorning the central hall and the antique gilded celadon vase on the sandalwood table, together with the old man in his cotton clothes sweeping the courtyard, all seem to remind us of a misty long past."

◎ 变身成茶庄的四落大厝。（康伦恩 摄）
The Four-Compound Mansion is a tea house now. (Photo by Kang Lun'en)

◎ 俯瞰四落大厝。（林乔森 摄）
Bird's eye view of Four—Compound Mansion. (Photo by Lin Qiaosen)

■ 四落大厝

　　这是舒婷笔下的闽南古厝，现鼓浪屿中华路23号、25号、海坛路33号、35号至39号的四落大厝。这四座院落是鼓浪屿现存规模最大、保存最完整的一组闽南红砖厝建筑群，占地面积3,100多平方米，建筑面积1,600多平方米，亦是岛上现存最古老的建筑群之一。

　　列入鼓浪屿遗产要素的四落大厝，是指鼓浪屿的原住民聚落——岩仔脚聚落留存下来的四组红砖厝建筑物组合的民间建筑。它们建于19世纪20至40年代，即清嘉庆、道光年间，由来自同安石浔的黄氏家族的黄有山、黄勗斋、黄崑石祖孙三代及族人修建。四落大厝布局遵循中国传统风水理念，靠山面海，中轴对称、一正两厢，建筑细部有砖作、石作、木作、彩绘等，淋漓尽致地表现出闽南红砖厝的中国传统文化底蕴。

　　饶有趣味的是，四落大厝有两个院落内的建筑被改造为近代洋楼样式。这也是19世纪中叶以来外来文化对鼓浪屿传统居住文化及建筑形式影响的佐证之一。

■ Four-Compound Mansion

These descriptions by Shu Ting, a well-known contemporary local female writer, are about the South Fujian Style ancient residential complexes with four adjacent compounds, located nowadays at 23, 25 Zhonghua Road, 33 and 35—39 of Haitan Road, Kulangsu. The complex is, as of now, the largest and best preserved group of red brick residences of South Fujian Style as well as one of the oldest existing complexes on the island, covering an area of more than 3,100m^2 with a floor space of more than 1,600m^2.

The Four-Compound Mansion, which is included in the heritage listings of Kulangsu, refers to the aboriginal architecture preserved at Yanzijiao (foot of the rock), composed of four groups of red brick buildings. They were built in the 1820s to 1840s by three generations of the three sons of the Huang family, namely, Huang Youshan, Huang Xuzhai and Huang Kunshi, together with their clansmen. Following the traditional Chinese idea of feng shui or geomancy, the mansion was backed by hills and faced the sea with a layout symmetrical about a central-axis. Each compound is comprised of a central hall, a master room and two wings. The construction itself is a masterpiece of brick, stone, wood and carvings, which exhibits the richness of traditional decorations in South Fujian.

Interestingly, two of these compounds were later converted into modern Western-style buildings. This is one of many examples of foreign influence on Kulangsu's traditional residential culture and architectural styles since the mid-19th century.

◎ 四落大厝之一 ——中华路25号院落。（康伦恩 摄）
The compound at 25 Zhonghua Road, one of Four-Compound Mansion. (Photo by Kang Lun'en)

◎ 俯瞰大夫第。（康伦恩 摄）
Bird's eye view of Dafudi Mansion. (Photo by Kang Lun'en)

■ 大夫第

　　距离四落大厝不远的大夫第（现海坛路58号），由一座两落五开间大厝和两排护厝组成，大厝前有较大的厝埕（庭院）。大夫第建于19世纪初，建筑占地面积1,300多平方米，建筑面积400多平方米，也是黄氏家族的黄勗斋及族人所建，是鼓浪屿现存最古老的红砖厝民居之一。

■ Dafudi Mansion

A short distance away from the Four-Compound Mansion is Dafudi Mansion (now at 58 Haitan Road), composed of a large primary building and two wings. The central building is made of five bays and a spacious courtyard. Built in the early 19th century by Huang Xuzhai and the clansmen of the Huang family, Dafudi covers an area of over 1,300m² and a floor space of more than 400m². It is one of the oldest red-brick residential dwellings on Kulangsu today.

◎ 修缮完好的大夫第。（康伦恩 摄）
Dafudi Mansion in good repair. (Photo by Kang Lun'en)

■ 黄氏小宗

从同安迁居鼓浪屿的黄姓是开发鼓浪屿的大家族之一，他们于元代初期定居在鼓浪屿的岩仔脚，后人有称其为"岩仔脚黄"的说法。黄姓的一个支系在岩仔脚建了祠堂——黄氏小宗（现市场路66号）。

黄氏小宗建于19世纪上半叶，一进院落，正房三开间，原建筑南侧有护厝，有着闽南风格的燕尾脊屋顶，是鼓浪屿现存最早的闽南传统木构红砖民居之一。经历一百多年的沧海桑田，现在的黄氏小宗仅余砖木结构的院门和正房，院门的条石门框上方嵌有"黄氏小宗"石匾。这座看似朴素不起眼的小院落，却记载了几段与鼓浪屿有关的重要历史。据申遗官方文本认定：1842年，美国归正教牧师雅裨理初到鼓浪屿，便是租住在当时还是海边院落的黄氏小宗里。雅裨理当时还兼任福建布政使徐继畬与英国首任驻厦门领事会晤的通译。雅裨理向徐继畬赠送了世界地理图册、地球仪，并向徐描述了一些美国、欧洲各国的状况。徐继畬以此为基础，再与各国来华人士交流后，写出《瀛寰志略》一书。

其后，黄氏族人也曾利用黄氏小宗开设私塾。1898年戊戌变法后，私塾改名为"普育小学堂"。

◎ 黄氏小宗。（康伦恩 摄）
Huang's Ancestral Hall. (Photo by Kang Lun'en)

■ Huang's Ancestral Hall

The Huang family, who moved here from Tong'an, is one of the major families who developed Kulangsu. They settled down at Yanzijiao in the early Yuan Dynasty and were therefore referred to as "Huang of Yanzijiao" by some later generations. A branch of the Huang family built an ancestral temple in the place and named it Huang's Ancestral Hall (now at 66 Market Road).

Built in the first half of the 19th century, Huang's Ancestral Hall was once a compound consisting of a three-bay central room and a south wing. With a dovetail ridge roof typical of South Fujian Style, it is one of the oldest existing traditional wood and red brick buildings on Kulangsu. Now, the century-old ancestral hall has only its gate of brick and wood and central room, together with a stone tablet with the characters of *Huang's Ancestral Hall* embedded above the ashlar door frame. Although the building was small, it was crucial for several landmark events in the island's history. According to official records, in 1842, David Abeel, a missionary of the American Reformed Church, arrived at Kulangsu and rented the building to preach. David Abeel was also appointed as an interpreter at the meeting between deputy governor of Fujian Xu Jiyu and Britain's first consul in Amoy. Abeel introduced Xu Jiyu to the wider global community and provided various geographical materials. It was with these documents and contact with other foreign people coming to China that Xu was able to write *Short Records of the World* (*Yinghuan Zhilüe*).

Later, the Huang family also established a private school at this place. After China's Reform Movement in 1898, it was renamed "Puyu (Universal) Elementary School".

◎ 艺术家在黄氏小宗内吹奏乐器。（康伦恩 摄）
An artist was performing on a musical instrument at Huang's Ancestral Hall. (Photo by Kang Lun'en)

殖民地外廊风格建筑

　　19世纪中叶，外国人进入鼓浪屿后，最初只能像传教的雅裨理牧师一样，租用民房。他们随后开始建造自己的领事馆、教堂、学校、医院、洋行和住宅等。鼓浪屿有欧式别墅的历史始于1844年，英国驻厦门第二任领事阿礼国着手在鼓浪屿鹿礁顶修建两幢领事办公楼（现鹿礁路14号、16号）。

◎ 绿树掩映下的美国领事馆旧址。（林乔森 摄）
Former US Consulate framed by green trees. (Photo by Lin Qiaosen)

　　此后，外国人在鼓浪屿占据风景优美之地，大兴土木。除了协和礼拜堂等少数几座例外，外国人在鼓浪屿兴建的建筑基本上都是殖民地外廊式建筑，此种建筑的风格便是具有休闲功能外廊空间。殖民地外廊式建筑形成于南亚殖民地区，又于18世纪末19世纪初传回欧洲，并成为富裕阶层的郊野别墅样式。殖民地外廊式建筑的建造成本相对西方古典建筑低，周期短，技术相对简便，加上又与亚太、非洲等热带、亚热带气候相适应，因此成为西方各国驻亚太、非洲殖民地公馆、住宅等建筑常用的形式。因此，鸦片战争前后，殖民地外廊式建筑便经英国在东南亚的殖民地传入中国，成为中国近代建筑最初的主要建筑样式。

Veranda Colonial Architectural Style

Upon coming to Kulangsu in the mid-19th century, foreigners initially rented local residences like Abeel did, before building their own consulates, churches, schools, hospitals, shops and mansions.

European-style villas on Kulangsu began to appear in 1844 when Sir. Rutherford Alcock, the second British Consul in Amoy, started the construction of two consular offices on the top of Lujiao Reef (now at 14 and 16, Lujiao Road).

Since then, foreigners have taken up construction projects in and around scenic areas of the island. With the exception of Union Church and a few other buildings, most were built in Veranda Colonial Style, of which the veranda was a place for leisure activities. This architectural style came into being in colonies in South Asia, and was introduced to Europe in country villas for the rich in the late 18th century and early 19th century. Compared to Western Classical Style buildings, this kind of building features lower costs, shorter construction periods, simpler techniques, and is suitable for the tropical and sub-tropical climate of the Asia-Pacific region and Africa. As a result, it became a very common architectural style for foreigners' mansions at the colonies in Asia-Pacific and Africa. Around the time of the Opium War, the Veranda Colonial Style was introduced to China by British people from their colonies in Southeast Asia to become a major architectural style of early Chinese architecture in modern times.

◎ 英国领事馆现已成为鼓浪屿历史文化陈列馆。（康伦恩 摄）
Former British Consulate has become Kulangsu Museum of History and Culture. (Photo by Kang Lun'en)

◎ 姑娘楼。（康伦恩 摄）
The Ladies' House. (Photo by Kang Lun'en)

■ 姑娘楼

现鸡山路1号的英国伦敦差会女传教士宅，曾是原伦敦差会专供女牧师、女教士居住的住宅，因其中多为终身未嫁的女传教士，所以被鼓浪屿居民俗称为"姑娘楼"。该建筑兴建于1856年之前，采用矩形平面，四周环绕宽阔的外廊空间，是典型的单层殖民地外廊式建筑。建筑基座部分是半层高、带券廊的防潮层，上部环绕着新文艺复兴风格的连续半圆拱券廊。"姑娘楼"亦是鼓浪屿现存最古老的建筑之一，它的圆拱长廊仍是旧时模样，老照片里那些女传教士坐在回廊里喝下午茶的情形，似乎就在昨日，也并不遥远。

■ The Ladies' House

Today's 1 Jishan Road used to be the residence of London Missionary Society for women. It was commonly referred to as "The Ladies' House" by locals because most residents were female missionaries who never married. The building, constructed before 1856, was a typical Veranda Colonial single-storey building of a rectangle courtyard surrounded by spacious verandas. The foundation includes a water-proof layer, above which is a semi-circular archway in Neo-Renaissance Style. As one of the oldest existing buildings on Kulangsu with its arched veranda kept intact, The Ladies' House always evokes imagination of women missionaries in old photos sitting on the veranda over a cup of afternoon tea. It all seems to have happened the day before, and not a distant past.

■ 廖家别墅

1919年，"脚踏中西文化"的文学大师林语堂，在鼓浪屿和钱庄老板廖悦发的二女儿廖翠凤结婚，新房便设在廖翠凤的家——廖家别墅之一（现漳州路44号）。廖家的两座别墅都是建于19世纪50年代的殖民地外廊式洋人住宅，被印尼归国华侨廖悦发购下居住。廖悦发曾在厦门开办"豫丰钱庄"，代理"天一总局"的日常业务，投资房地产，参与投资鼓浪屿淘化大同公司等多家企业。出身漳州乡间贫穷牧师家庭的林语堂，10岁来到鼓浪屿的教会学校求学，后来在上海圣约翰大学求学时恋上同学的妹妹，岛上医生、富商陈天恩的女儿陈锦端，却爱而不得，最后被不嫌弃他穷困、陈家隔邻的廖家二小姐相中。廖家二小姐这个林语堂口中的"富有的银行家之女"和他携手相伴终生。

林语堂新婚所住的这幢别墅，平面呈"凹"字形，因地势较低，设置了较高的防潮层，建筑主入口前修建了很高的大台阶。建筑的外廊空间正面为新文艺复兴风格的连续圆拱外廊，外廊上部可以看到后面大面的三角形山墙。外廊空间后面是建筑矩形平面的主体部分，中间是贯通前后的回廊，两侧是房间。廖家另一幢别墅（现漳州路48号）高两层，原名"立人斋"，圆拱长廊，现已残破。廖家别墅也是鼓浪屿上"年岁最大"的别墅之一。站在院落里，想象着当年的傻小子林语堂新婚那天，把甜茶里作为象征之用的莲子、龙眼全吃了；想象着他携带妻女应林文庆之邀，到厦门大学任教，住回此楼，廖翠凤下厨请同在厦门大学任教的鲁迅吃家宴……一百年的光阴流转，这些情景只能在林语堂的笔下重现了。

值得一提的是中国工程院院士、著名呼吸病学专家，抗击非典和新型冠状病毒肺炎的重要人物钟南山与廖家的关系匪浅。钟南山的母亲廖月琴就出自鼓浪屿廖家。廖月琴的爷爷廖天赐与廖家别墅主人廖悦发是亲兄弟。同时，钟南山出身医学世家，父亲钟世藩是儿科专家，母亲廖月琴毕业于协和医学院，舅舅舅妈，姨夫姨妈也都是医生和护士。

◎ 廖家别墅之一——立人斋。（康伦恩 摄）
"Li Ren Zhai (Mind-Cultivating House)", one of Liao Family Villas. (Photo by Kang Lun'en)

■ Liao Family Villas

In 1919, Lin Yutang, a famous modern Chinese writer known to be "a bridge between Chinese and Western cultures", married Liao Cuifeng, second daughter of a private banker Liao Yuefa. The wedding chamber was in the bride's house, one of Liao Family Villas (now at 44 Zhangzhou Road). Both villas were built in the 1850s in Veranda Colonial Style, and were later purchased by Liao Yuefa, a returned overseas Chinese businessman from Indonesia. He established "Yufeng Qianzhuang", an old-style Chinese private bank, and handled the daily business of the Tianyi General Office as an agent. He also invested in real estate development and held shares of Amoy Food Limited and other companies.

Born into a poor priest family in the countryside of Zhangzhou, Fujian Province, Lin Yutang began his education in a missionary school on Kulangsu at the age of 10. He fell in love when he was a college student at Saint John's University, Shanghai, with Chen Jinduan, younger sister of his classmate and daughter of a wealthy businessman Chen Tian'en who was also a doctor on the island. Although this love was fruitless, Lin found his true love, Liao Cuifeng, "daughter of a rich banker", who happened to be a neighbor of the Chen family, and the marriage turned out to be a very happy one.

The villa where Lin Yutang and his newly-wed wife lived was concave in shape and was built with a higher moisture proof layer than usual to compensate for its low altitude, which also resulted in many steps at the main entrance of the building. The front of the villa was Neo-Renaissance styled, wtih continuous arched verandas with large triangular pediments. Behind the veranda was the main section of the building, and the interconnected corridors in the middle were flanked by rows of rooms. The other villa of the Liao family, a two-storey building (now at 48 Zhangzhou Road) named "Li Ren Zhai (Mind-Cultivating House)", is also in veranda style but has now fallen into disrepair. The two villas of the Liao family are also among the oldest on the island. Standing in the courtyard, one may think about how muddle-headed younger Lin Yutang, on his wedding day, ate up all the lotus seed and longan in the sweet tea served which are symbolic of fertility and are not supposed to be eaten up; and how he later came back to live in this building with his wife and daughters and taught at Amoy University at the invitation of the then president Lim Boon Keng; and how Lu Xun, another renowned modern Chinese writer who was also teaching at the university at the time, was invited to family dinners prepared by Liao Cuifeng... These little moments of daily life happening about a century ago are known only to us because of Lin's writings.

It is worth mentioning that Zhong Nanshan, an academician of the Chinese Academy of Engineering, a famous respiratory expert and a major specialist in the fight against SARS and COVID-19, has a close tie with the Liao family. Zhong's mother, Liao Yueqin, is from the Liao family on Kulangsu. Liao Yueqin's grandfather Liao Tianci and Liao Yuefa, the owner of Liao Family Villas, were brothers. At the same time, Zhong Nanshan was born into a medical family. His father Zhong Shifan is a pediatrician. His mother Liao Yueqin graduated from Peking Union Medical College. Many of his uncles and aunts are doctors or nurses.

◎ 廖家别墅。（康伦恩 摄）
Liao Family Villa. (Photo by Kang Lun'en)

■ 汇丰银行公馆

百年之前的情景在鼓浪屿或许还可以寻觅！在笔山的断崖之上俯瞰海天的汇丰银行公馆（现鼓新路57号）建于1876年，最初是英商怡记洋行的闲乐居，后成为汇丰银行行长的住宅。汇丰银行公馆为单层砖木结构，前后设有外廊，廊柱用特制弧形红砖砌筑，建筑平面则为特殊的三叶草形。1873年，英国"香港上海汇丰银行"在厦门开设分行，为厦门最早的近代银行。坐在复原的别墅厅堂里，或者阔大的长廊上，喝喝下午茶，脚下的花砖虽然经历了近一百五十年岁月的磨损，也仍然有着颜色与花纹，举目远眺厦鼓两岸风光，别有一番逸趣。而隔邻的建造时间不晚于1927年的汇丰银行职工公寓，清水红砖，造型简洁，屋内的木头栏杆和地板都是旧日模样。站在回廊上，山风与海风激荡，在某个刹那间，足以使当年寓居岛上的异乡人忘却烦恼吧？

◎ 汇丰银行公馆旧址。（杨戈 摄）
Former residence of HSBC's President. (Photo by Yang Ge)

■ Former Residence of HSBC's President

The landscape of one hundred years ago could still be seen on Kulangsu today! The former Residence of HSBC's President on the cliff of Bishan Hill (now at 57 Guxin Road) is one of such sights. Built in 1876 and providing an incredible view of the sea, the residence first served as a leisure house of former Messrs. Elles & Company and later became HSBC's President's residence. It is a single-storey brick-wood structure with a cloverleaf layout featuring surrounding veranda at the front and back, together with curved red brick columns. It was in 1873 that HSBC branched out in Amoy and set up the first modern bank in Xiamen.

Just think what a unique and relaxing experience it would be to sit in the hall of the renovated villa or by the broad veranda over a cup of afternoon tea. Under your feet are tiles which, though wearing away by exposure to the elements for nearly 150 years, still have their colors and patterns. Looking afar, one could be enchanted by the pretty scenery of Kulangsu and Amoy across the Lujiang Strait. The neighboring house is the former staff residence of HSBC built no later than 1927, with fair-faced red bricks and a rather simple design. The wooden railings and floors look the same as they were a century before. Standing on the veranda admist the breeze from the hill and the sea, one may forget worldly worries and enjoy peace of mind.

◎ 建于悬崖之上的汇丰银行公馆。（林乔森 摄）
Residence of HSBC's President on the cliff. (Photo by Lin Qiaosen)

◎ 万国俱乐部旧址。（子健传媒 供图）
Former Amoy Club. (Courtesy of Zijian Media)

■ 万国俱乐部

　　不过要让人忘却烦恼，还得有日常丰富之娱乐。鼓浪屿上曾有的洋人俱乐部，在20世纪20年代初被华侨黄秀烺购买后建起海天堂构，俱乐部则迁址至田尾东路临近海滨的坡地。新建的万国俱乐部（现田尾路8号）也被称为"群乐楼"，建筑面积1,541平方米，为砖混结构。两层高的殖民地外廊式建筑，已具有一定现代建筑特征，造型简洁，内设舞厅、酒吧、台球室、保龄球室、外文书籍阅览室与交际厅等。万国俱乐部是当时鼓浪屿上的外国人、华人富绅、洋行高级雇员娱乐交际的场所，人们在此觥筹交错，好不热闹。

■ Former Amoy Club

Entertainment facilities added to the fun. What used to be Foreigners' Club was purchased by overseas Chinese Huang Xiulang in the early 1920s to have Hai Tian Tang Gou Mansion built. The club moved to a hill near the seaside of East Tianwei Road and was rebuilt to become former Amoy Club (now at 8 Tianwei Road). Also known as All Joy Club, the site covers a floor space of more than 1,541m^2 and is a two-storey brick-concrete structure in Veranda Colonial Style with modern architectural features of simplicity and functionality, including a ballroom, a bar, a billiard saloon, a bowling alley, a reading room with foreign books and a function hall. The club served as a very popular place for foreigners, rich Chinese, senior Chinese employees of foreign companies to socialize and enjoy themselves.

■ 大北电报公司办公楼

1871年初，在笔架山的另一边，当年视线所及的海边，丹麦人建造起了大北电报公司的办公楼，并将香港至上海的海底电缆引线至建筑内，开始收发电报。丹麦大北电报公司办公楼（现田尾路21号）也是单层殖民地外廊式建筑，砖木结构，矩形平面，南北两侧为连续的圆拱外廊。如今静静伫立于海边，听着海潮拍案的丹麦大北电报公司办公楼是中国最早收发电报的场所之一。作为离岛的鼓浪屿能与海外许多国家建立联系，在商贸与文化的交流上毫无障碍，这座朴素的楼宇亦有功劳。

■ Former Office Building of Great Northern Telegraph Company (Denmark)

In early 1871, on the other side of Bijia Hill and by an expanse of sea as far as the eye could see, the Danish had their Great Northern Telegraph Company (Denmark) office building constructed and connected to submarine cables linked to Hong Kong and Shanghai so they could begin to send and receive telegrams. The office building (now at 21 Tianwei Road) is also a single-storey brick and wood structure in Veranda Colonial Style with a rectangular courtyard and continuous arched verandas running along its south and north sides. Standing silently by the sea and listening to the waves rolling in, the former office of the Great Northern Telegraph Company was one of the earliest operators in China offering telegram services and had enabled the outlying Kulangsu to establish commercial and cultural ties with many countries.

◎ 丹麦大北电报公司旧址。（子健传媒 供图）
Former Office of Great Northern Telegraph Company (Denmark). (Courtesy of Zijian Media)

■ 英商亚细亚火油公司

跨洋而来、从事商贸而获得丰厚回报的还有英商亚细亚火油公司。亚细亚火油公司1903年7月于伦敦成立，接着在上海成立中国总部，曾垄断亚洲、特别是20世纪上半叶的中国销售市场。该公司销售的产品最初为煤油，后又增加汽油、柴油、航空燃料、重油、润滑油、沥青、石蜡等。鼓浪屿上的英商亚细亚火油公司旧址（现中华路21号）是一座两层殖民地外廊式建筑，采用了英国维多利亚时期具有代表性的清水红砖及哥特式尖券拱窗。因其窗洞特别像圆睁双眼的猫头鹰，鼓浪屿人又称其为"猫头鹰楼"，是颇具趣味的一幢老别墅。

■ **Former Office Building of British Asiatic Petroleum Company**

Also coming to trade with China across the ocean and reaping high profits was the British Asiatic Petroleum Company. Founded in London in July 1903, the company set up its Chinese headquarters in Shanghai and had monopolized the oil market in Asia, especially in China, during the first half of the 20th century by selling kerosene, gasoline, diesel, aviation fuel, thick oil, lubricant, asphalt, petrolatum and other petroleum products. The former Office Building of the British Asiatic Petroleum Company on Kulangsu (now at 21 Zhonghua Road) was a two-storey Veranda Colonial Style building, with fair faced red brick walls and Gothic pointed arched windows which were styled after Victorian England. It was an interesting old villa, sometimes called "the owl building" by locals because it had windows that looked exactly like an owl with opened eyes.

◎ 英商亚细亚火油公司旧址。（康伦恩 摄）
Former Office Building of the British Asiatic Petroleum Company. (Photo by Kang Lun'en)

◎ 英商亚细亚火油公司独具特色的"猫头鹰窗"。（康伦恩 摄）
One of the "owl windows" of former Office Building of the British Asiatic Petroleum Company. (Photo by Kang Lun'en)

■ 英国领事公馆

　　高居开阔之地、直面鹭江两岸的英国领事公馆（现漳州路5号），是鼓浪屿上第一座领事公馆。1878年，英国驻厦门代理领事翟理斯上任，英国领事机构由"领事事务所"级别升至"领事馆"级别，人员扩编，业务量增大，因此购买这幢原为德国洋行所有的建筑作为领事馆办公人员的居所。英国领事公馆初建为两层，后来改建成现状的一层，为典型的单层殖民地外廊式建筑，砖石木结构，建筑平面为"L"形，外侧设置外廊空间。"L"形长边外廊内侧设置卧室，短边外廊内侧设置厅堂，厅堂后面是厨卫等辅助房间，住在此地，可真算得上是住在风景里。此楼20世纪80年代重建，已非原样。

■ Former Residence of British Consulate

Sitting at spacious higher ground overlooking Kulangsu and Amoy across the Lujiang Strait, the former Residence of British Consulate (now at 5 Zhangzhou Road) was the first residence of a foreign consul on the island. In 1878, Herbert Allen Giles was appointed British acting consul in Amoy as the Consular Office was upgraded to the Consulate. With an increase in staff members and business, the British Consulate purchased the building which was once owned by a German firm as the residence for consulate staff. The building originally had two storeys and was later renovated to the current one-storey structure in typical Veranda Colonial Style built of brick, stone and wood. In the shape of "L", the building features protruding eternal verandas, internal bedrooms and the main hall with auxiliary rooms such as kitchen and bathrooms at the back. The building was rebuilt in the 1980s and is not what it used to be.

◎ 英国领事公馆旧址。（康伦恩 摄）
Former Residence of British Consulate. (Photo by Kang Lun'en)

■ 美国领事馆

　　除英国外，美国是最早派驻厦门领事的国家。现存的原美国领事馆（现三明路26号）翻建于20世纪30年代，位于三丘田海滨，由美国建筑师设计，是一座殖民地外廊式的二层建筑。建筑平面呈"H"形，朝海的东侧凹入处设置外廊，采用六根乳白色古希腊科林斯柱式的巨柱，柱头花纹为百合花装饰，红砖实墙砌筑建筑两翼，建筑的主色调为紫红和乳白。美国领事馆总占地6,300平方米，花园巨大，由于地势较高，又面向鹭江，厦鼓风光，一览无余。美国领事馆旧址是20世纪上半叶鼓浪屿领事馆建筑的代表，见证着一座不足两平方千米的小岛曾有13个国家领事馆的历史。

■ Former US Consulate

Following shortly after the UK, the US appointed a consul to Amoy very early on. The existing former US Consulate (now at 26 Sanming Road), renovated in the 1930s and located on the coast of Sanqiutian, was a two-storey Veranda Colonial Style building designed by an American architect. The building plane was in the shape of "H", with the veranda built at the recess of the eastern side facing the sea. Six huge ivory Corinthian columns supported and adorned the veranda, each decorated with lilies at the top. The building had its two wings made of solid red bricks but the dominant tone was fuchsia and milky white. Located on higher ground and covering an area of 6,300m² with a spacious garden, the Consulate faced the Lujiang Strait and enjoyed a very good view of Amoy and Kulangsu.

The former US Consulate is a prime example of the consulate buildings on Kulangsu in the first half of the 20th century, a witness of a glorious past of 13 consulates on a small island less than two square kilometers.

◎ 日本领事馆旧址。（林乔森 摄）
Former Japanese Consulate. (Photo by Lin Qiaosen)

■ 日本领事馆和日本警察署及其宿舍

完好地保存下来的领事馆还有建于19世纪末的日本领事馆（现鹿礁路24号）。采用木屋架的日本领事馆，建筑形式同样是19世纪末在中国开埠城镇流行的殖民地外廊样式，两层建筑的立面均设置了连续的半圆拱券，清水红砖外墙，砌砖工艺采用标准的英式砌法。1902年1月10日，厦门兴泉永道道台延年、日本领事兼领袖领事上野专一、英国领事满思礼、美国领事费思洛等中外各国代表便是在这座日本领事馆建筑内签署了《厦门鼓浪屿公共地界章程》。

与日本领事馆相邻的日本警察署及其宿舍（现鹿礁路26号、28号），作为日本领事馆的附属设施，建于1928年。日本警察署的建筑为钢筋砖混结构，中轴对称，建筑立面强调竖向线条，具有当时风靡美国及东亚城市的装饰艺术风格特征。警察署宿舍则是具有早期现代建筑风格特征的建筑，宿舍内部居住单元保留有部分当时日式风格的室内装饰。警察署地下原设有监狱，监狱的墙上还留有当年被关押者的手书。在这座岛屿最黑暗的时刻，建筑也以自己的方式保留历史的记忆。

■ Former Japanese Consulate, Japanese Police Station and Staff Quarters

Well-preserved foreign consulates on Kulangsu also include former Japanese Consulate (now at 24 Lujiao Road) built at the end of the 19th century. With timber roof trusses, the building was also in Veranda Colonial Style which was popular in Chinese cities opening as commercial ports at the end in 19th century. The front of the two-storey building was set with continuous semicircular arched verandas, and the external wall of fairfaced red brick was finished with British bricklaying workmanship. On January 10, 1902, representatives of China and foreign countries, including Yannian, Commissioner of Xinghua-Quanzhou-Yongchun Administration based in Amoy, Senichi Uyeno, Japanese Consul and the consul general, R. W. Mansfield, British consul and John H. Fesler, American consul, signed *Land Regulations for the Settlement of Kulangsu, Amoy*, in this Japanese Consulate.

The former Japanese Police Station and Staff Quarters (now at 26 and 28 Lujiao Road), the auxiliary amenities of the Japanese Consulate, were constructed in 1928. The Police Station was a reinforced concrete building symmetrical around a central-axis with vertical lines on the façade, a Deco Style popular in American and East Asian cities. The Staff Quarters feature early modernist architecture, and apartments within the Quarters retain the Japanese-style interior decoration of the time. The Police Station used to have a jail underground, and the prisoners' scribbles on the wall are still visible. On the island's darkest moments, the architecture has in its own way helped preserve history.

◎ 日本警察署旧址。（子健传媒 供图）
Former Japanese Police Station. (Courtesy of Zijian Media)

■ 厦门海关

晚清的中国海关由外国人执掌，雇用了许多外籍人员。厦门海关也在鼓浪屿兴建了不少建筑，比如建于1923年的厦门海关验货员公寓（现中华路2号）便是20世纪上半叶鼓浪屿殖民地外廊式建筑中的精品。此楼被鼓浪屿人称为"白鼠楼"，是厦门海关安置外籍验货员的高级公寓。公寓为两层五单元连排式集合住宅，可安置五户验货员家庭在此居住生活，因由相对独立的五个单元组成，原编的门牌号也是五个，鼓浪屿人也称之为"五间排"。厦门海关还在附近建造了海关副税务司公馆（现漳州路9号、11号）。两幢别墅造型简洁洗练，明显受到当时现代建筑风潮的影响，带有美国草原别墅风格。另有现存的理船厅公所（现鼓新路60号）为厦门海关1883年购入的产业，1914年扩展形成现在的格局，为当时厦门海关理船厅公馆与办公建筑。理船厅公所以红白两色对比为主调，风格轻巧而不失秀丽。

◎ 海关理船厅公所旧址。
（子健传媒 供图）
Former Amoy Maritime Affairs Office. (Courtesy of Zijian Media)

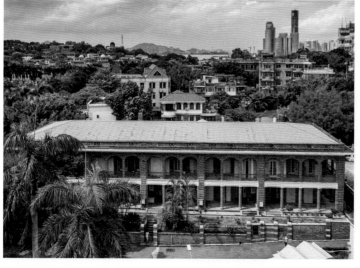

◎ 海关验货员公寓旧址。
（林乔森 摄）
Former Amoy Customs Inspectors' Quarters. (Photo by Lin Qiaosen)

◎ 厦门海关副税务司公馆旧址。（林乔森 摄）
Former Residence of Amoy Customs Deputy Commissioner. (Photo by Lin Qiaosen)

■ Amoy Customs

Chinese customs in the late Qing Dynasty was run by foreigners and there were many foreign employees. To accommodate these people, Amoy Customs had many apartments built on Kulangsu. Among them, the former Amoy Customs Inspectors' Quarters (now at 2 Zhonghua Road) was a masterpiece in Veranda Colonial Style popular on the island in the first half of the 20th century. The deluxe accommodation, built for foreign customs inspectors, was a two-storey apartment building for five families, which was also referred to as "Five-apartment Building" ("Wujianpai" in Chinese) by locals because it consisted of five independent apartments with separate house numbers. Amoy Customs also had the Residence of Amoy Customs Deputy Commissioner built nearby (now at 9 and 11 Zhangzhou Road). Simple but sophisticated in the style of American prairie villa, the two residences were obviously influenced by modern architectural trends of the time. The existing former Maritime Affairs Office (now at 60 Guxin Road) was another building belonging to Amoy Customs, which was purchased in 1883 and expanded to the current structure in 1914. It functioned as both residence and office building, built using a nice contrast of red and white.

　　在华侨归国定居鼓浪屿的热潮开始之前，岛上先期发家致富的当地人，也已经建起殖民地外廊风格的别墅。比如建于1902年的白登弼宅的南楼（现复兴路98号）便是鼓浪屿中国居民早期自建的殖民地外廊式住宅。白登弼因与教会合作，其印刷企业"萃经堂"生意兴隆，后参与投资"淘化罐头厂"。建于1908年的吴添丁阁，原为著名音乐家殷承宗祖父的私宅，曾借给教会办学，是蒙学堂的第二校址，后被菲律宾华侨吴添丁购买。该建筑是一座二层的殖民地外廊式建筑，风格简朴，坐北朝南，南面上下两层均设外廊，为连续七个圆拱券的新文艺复兴风格券廊，院墙的装饰中则采用了中国传统园林的花漏窗及吉祥图案装饰。

■ Wu Tianding's Mansion

Even before Kulangsu became a popular place to settle down for overseas Chinese returning to their motherland, several rich local residents had had their own villas in Veranda Colonial Style built. One typical example is the South Building of Bai Dengbi Mansion built in 1902 (now at 98 Fuxing Road). Bai Dengbi ran a printshop named "Cuijing House" and had been doing very well in cooperation with the church. He was also one of the investors in Amoy Food Limited. Another example is Wu Tianding's Mansion (Mengxuetang), which was established in 1908 on what used to be private residence of the grandfather of Yin Chengzong, a very famous Chinese musician and pianist who was born on Kulangsu. The premises were first lent to a church to be used as a school, namely Mengxuetang, and later bought by Philippine overseas Chinese Wu Tianding. A two-storey house in Veranda Colonial Style facing south and simple in style, the building was designed with protruding verandas and seven Neo-Renaissance styled porches on both floors. The walls of the house were adorned with lattice windows and auspicious patterns typical of traditional Chinese gardens.

◎ 吴添丁阁。（子健传媒 供图）
Wu Tianding's Mansion. (Courtesy of Zijian Media)

◎ 协和礼拜堂。（康伦恩 摄）
Union Church. (Photo by Kang Lun'en)

西方古典复兴风格及其他风格建筑

虽然19世纪中叶到20世纪初，鼓浪屿上兴建的建筑基本是殖民地外廊式风格，但其中也有几个例外，在岛上遍布的殖民地外廊式建筑中显得独树一帜。

■ 各式教堂

英美三公会于1863年在鼓浪屿的鹿耳礁建起了一座鼓浪屿始建年代最早的教堂——西方古典复兴风格的协和礼拜堂（现福建路60号），提供给来鼓浪屿工作的外籍基督教人士作基督教专用英语礼拜所用，后来懂英语的中国教徒也被吸纳其中。

建于1917年的天主教堂（现鹿礁路34号），为哥特式单钟楼教堂。教堂建筑平面为巴西礼卡式，四个尖拱构成大厅空间，南侧入口处有一座哥特式钟塔，装饰着华丽的尖券门窗及玫瑰窗，是厦门地区仅存的一座哥特式天主教堂。

◎ 天主堂。（杨戈 摄）
Catholic Church. (Photo by Yang Ge)

Western Classical Revival Architecture and Other Styles

Although buildings of Veranda Colonial Style prevailed in the period between the mid-19th and early 20th centuries on Kulangsu, there were exceptions which presented different and diverse styles on the island.

■ Churches of Different Styles

For instance, the Union Church (now at 60 Fujian Road) of Classical Revival Style was one of the earliest chapels on Kulangsu. Established at Lu'erjiao in 1863 by the Three Societies co-founded by the American Reformed Church, London Missionary Society and British Presbyterian Church, it used to be a place exclusively for foreign Christians working on Kulangsu to attend religious services in English. Later, English-speaking Chinese Christians also joined in.

Built in 1917, the Catholic Church (now at 34 Lujiao Road) was of Gothic Style and laid out in a Basilica design. Four cusped arches constitute the hall space and a gothic bell tower stands at the south entrance, decorated with ornate gothic doors and windows with pointed arches and rose windows. The building is now the only existing Catholic church of the Gothic Style in the Amoy region.

■ 博爱医院

　　1935年，博爱医院（现鹿礁路1号）经第三次迁址，在鼓浪屿的鹿礁路建起新的医院大楼。博爱医院是20世纪30年代厦门医疗设备最完善、技术力量最雄厚的大型综合性医疗机构。该楼占地面积11,354平方米，建筑面积4,700多平方米，由日本建筑师设计，建筑风格为20世纪30年代在日本国内开始风行的早期现代建筑形式。博爱医院采用"日"字形平面，有两处天井院，一处作为羽毛球场，一处是住院病患室外活动的空间。外墙面以浅米黄色涂刷与深米黄色釉面砖边缘装饰相配合，与建筑内部装修相呼应，体现出浓郁的日本风格。

◎ 博爱医院旧址。（康伦恩 摄）
Former Pok Oi Hospital. (Photo by Kang Lun'en)

■ **Former Pok Oi Hospital**

In 1935, Pok Oi Hospital (now at 1 Lujiao Road), the best equipped medical institution in the 1930s in Amoy, moved to its new premises at Lujiao Road, Kulangsu. This was the third relocation of the hospital and the new building covered an area of 11,354m², with a floor space of more than 4,700m². Designed by Japanese architects on a plane like the Chinese character "日" to better meet the functional requirements, the building was of the early modernist architectural style popular in Japan in the 1930s, with two open-air patios. One served as the badminton court of the hospital and the other for other outdoor activities for patients. As typical Japanese architecture, the external facade was painted with alternating light and dark beige to match the interior finish.

■ 三一堂

　　三一堂（现安海路67号）的建筑风格则是在20世纪初流行的西方古典复兴风格基础上做了适当简化，采用希腊十字平面，大厅内部无立柱，上部是八边形的屋顶。该教堂开建于1934年，1945年方大体竣工，其名寓意"圣父、圣子、圣灵三位一体"。教堂先由留洋工程师林荣廷主持设计，许春草负责施工，中途由于拓展规模导致原设计无法继续，又聘请荷兰工程师对建筑结构重新设计，并从香港定制屋顶的巨型钢架。这个原建于地瓜地之上的教堂，自1934年开建，2000年还扩建了教堂正门以及附属建筑、围墙栏杆等未了工程，整座教堂历时60多年才全部竣工，也算是一段曲折的故事。

■ Trinity Church

Trinity Church (now at 67 Anhai Road) was an example of a simplified Western Classical Revival Style popular in the early 20th century, laid out in Greek cross design with an octagonal ceiling. There were no pillar inside the hall. The church started construction in 1934 and was mostly completed in 1945. The name embodied the religious doctrine of the Trinity—the Father, the Son, and the Holy Spirit. The building was first designed by Lin Rongting, an engineer who studied overseas, and constructed by Xu Chuncao. Lin Rongting was unable to finish the task because of an interrupting expansion plan, so a Dutch engineer was brought in to redesign it and the huge steel frame on the roof had to be custom-made in Hong Kong. Sitting on sweet potato fields, the church was given its last touches in 2000 when the main entrance, annexes as well as fences and railings were built. We could even say that the construction of the church lasted over 60 years since 1934!

◎ 三一堂。（康伦恩 摄）
Trinity Church. (Photo by Kang Lun'en)

■ 安献堂

　　来自美国的基督复临安息日会，曾通过美国领事馆以低价买了公地，在鼓浪屿鸡山路、鼓声路一带陆续建造几幢楼房，其中之一就是作为讲经传道之用的安献堂（现鸡山路18号）。1934年，安息日会牧师安礼逊在鸡山顶兴建一座三层楼房，设计师是一位被称为"富师"的惠安建筑工匠。该建筑开山取花岗石建造，坐北朝南，矩形平面，平面格局为封闭式内廊布局。建筑对称的正立面中部设入口，首层为平台，大台阶直接引向设在二层的入口，设有突出的柱廊，柱廊由前面四根和靠墙两根巨大的石柱支撑。横三段的对称布局，高台阶，竖向三段式的立面划分，以及中部巨大的入口柱廊体现出古典复兴风格的影响。

　　安献堂如今是养老院。成为养老院的还有岛上的另一座教堂——福音堂（现晃岩路40号）。福音堂建于1903年，巨石筑砌的台基，入口为中式天井，硬山坡屋顶，山墙饰西式三角山花及藤蔓图案，设计巧妙，建筑稳固。

◎ 安献堂。（康伦恩 摄）
Anxian Hall. (Photo by Kang Lun'en)

◎ 福音堂。（杨戈 摄）

Gospel Hall. (Photo by Yang Ge)

■ Anxian Hall

Missionaries of the American Christian Seventh-Day Adventists Church had managed to purchase, via the US Consulate, a piece of public land at a low price, and had several houses built along Jishan Road and Gusheng (Drum Sound) Road. One of the buildings was "Anxian Hall" (now at 18 Jishan Road), which was used as a chapel for the Church. In 1934, the Rev. J. N. Anderson had a three-storey chapel built on the top of Jishan Hill and the designer was from South Fujian's Hui'an, known as "Fu Shi". The building was made of granite mined from the hill. Facing south, it had a rectangular base, with a closed corridor structure. An entrance was set in the middle of the symmetrical front facade. The first floor was a platform and the high staircases led directly to the entrance of the second floor where there was a protruding colonnade supported by four huge stone pillars at the front and two against the wall. All of the horizontal division, high staircases, three-section vertical division, and the huge entrance colonnade in the center are symmetrical as a result of the influence of the Classical Revival Style.

Anxian Hall has now transformed into gerocomium, as has Gospel Hall (now at 40 Huangyan Road), another former chapel on the island. Built in 1903, Gospel Hall was firmly based on a foundation of large stones, and the entrance was a Chinese patio with a hard hillside roof and a gable ingeniously decorated with Western pediments and vine designs.

"厦门装饰风格" 的萌发与兴盛

1895年，由台湾内渡鼓浪屿的林鹤年在鼓浪屿建起了寓所"怡园"（现福建路24号）。

林鹤年，祖籍安溪，晚清福建八大诗人之一，因日本人侵占台湾，不得已内渡鼓浪屿，却"心不忘台湾"而建怡园。怡园为厦门装饰风格，中式塌寿密缝红砖建筑，共三层(含地下防潮层)，石砌防潮层以上通体为密缝清水红砖墙面。怡园内留有清代书法家吕世宜所书的"小桃源"石刻，以及传说中郑成功开凿的井——"剑泉"。

在闽、台的富绅及闽籍华侨定居鼓浪屿的热潮中，鼓浪屿在多元文化交流的土壤中生发出具有本土建筑特征的"厦门装饰风格"。这种由西方古典复兴式、现代主义风格、装饰艺术风格融合生发出的建筑风格，呈现在华侨建造的具有本土特征的华侨洋楼、华侨家族宅园、私家园林中，并且成为鼓浪屿的"万国建筑"中华丽而珍贵的存在。有数据统计，仅1920年至1930年间，岛上由华侨组织建造的住宅就达1,041栋。

◎ 怡园。（杨戈 摄）
Yiyuan Garden. (Photo by Yang Ge)

◎ 黄家花园。（康伦恩 摄）

Huang Family Villa. (Photo by Kang Lun'en)

Popularization and Growth of the Amoy Deco Style

In 1895, Lin Henian from Taiwan had "Yiyuan Garden" (now at 24 Fujian Road) built on Kulangsu.

Lin Henian, one of the eight most famous Fujian poets in the late Qing Dynasty, had his ancestral home in Anxi of South Fujian. He settled down on Kulangsu because of the Japanese invasion of Taiwan and therefore built "Yiyuan Garden" to give expression to his nostalgia. The two-storey house based on a stone foundation is an all close-joint and fairfaced red-brick structure (including the facade) in Amoy Deco Style. In the mansion there are stone inscriptions of "Shangri-La in Miniature" written by Lyu Shiyi, a calligrapher of the Qing Dynasty, and "Sword Spring", the well dug by Koxinga hundreds of years ago.

While there was an increasing number of mansions constructed by rich people of Fujian and Taiwan, and overseas Chinese from Fujian settling down on Kulangsu, Amoy Deco Style, a localized architectural style, had its roots taken hold in the soil of cultural diversity. It is a combination of Western Classical Revival Style, Modernist Style and Art Deco Style together with local features typically found in houses, mansions and private gardens, which have been magnificent and valuable presence of the diversified architectural styles on Kulangsu. According to statistics, there were as many as 1,041 such dwellings built by overseas Chinese in the 1920s and 1930s.

◎ 林尔嘉与家人摄于菽庄花园。（陈亚元 供图）

Lin Erjia (Lim Nee Kar) and his family at Shuzhuang Garden Villa. (Courtesy of Chen Yayuan)

■ **菽庄花园**

　　从台湾内渡鼓浪屿的林尔嘉，"瞻望故园，萦回梦寐"，思念他少时在台北居住的江南式花园"板桥别墅"，遂在1913年的秋天，于鼓浪屿的东南海滨坡地上，"购得隙地，披荆斩棘、剪榛除莽，就其势之高低，因地制宜，为亭为阁，筑台筑榭，凿池凿沼"，仿照台北板桥别墅，造起了菽庄花园——他把这段故事，刻在园中的石头上。"板桥莫问当年事，重起楼台做主人"，别墅以他的字"叔臧"的谐音取名"菽庄"。

菊黄蟹肥时候，月亮晴好之夜，林尔嘉约了众多文人诗友，在园中谈瀛轩里、四十四桥上，听涛，赏月，吟诗。在有月亮的晚上，站在大海之中的四十四桥上看看风景，听听涛声琴音，是能让你对这借山藏海巧布局的园子生出些感叹的。扶栏观月、吟诗作对的风雅乐事，也是这座小岛骨子里的浪漫基因。而如今为游客所开辟的菽庄花园不仅是鼓浪屿最重要的私家园林，也是中国岭南地区最重要的近代园林之一。

◎ 林尔嘉把菽庄花园的故事刻在石头上。（康伦恩 摄）
Lin Erjia inscribed the story of Shuzhuang Garden Villa on the stone. (Photo by Kang Lun'en)

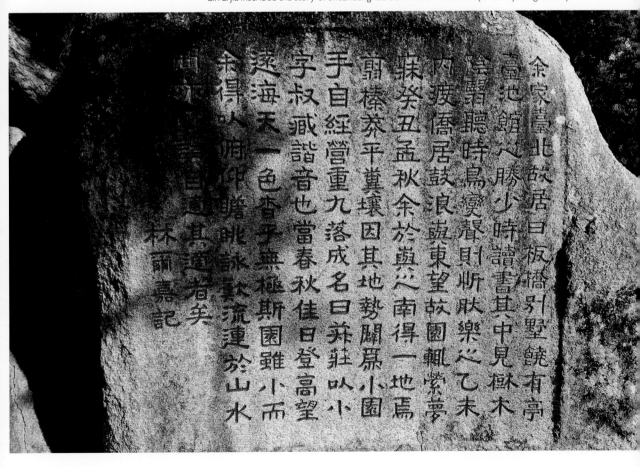

■ Shuzhuang Garden Villa

Lin Erjia (Lim Nee Kar) came to settle down on Kulangsu across the Straits from Taiwan but missed his family's "Banchiau Garden", a villa of South China Style in Taipei where he spent his childhood. To remember this, he bought a piece of land on the hillside at the southeast coast of Kulangsu and had Shuzhuang Garden Villa built in the autumn of 1913, following the style of Lin family's Banchiau Garden and ingeniously adjusted the design to the features of the terrain. He inscribed this memory on one of the rocks in the garden and named the place "Shuzhuang" (literally meaning "Bean Plantation" in Chinese) after his courtesy name "Shuzang", a homophone to "Shuzhuang".

◎ 借山藏海的菽庄花园。（康伦恩 摄）
Shuzhuang Garden Villa in between the hill and the sea. (Photo by Kang Lun'en)

◎ 菽庄花园兼具中式园林之美。（康伦恩 摄）

Shuzhuang Garden Villa: incorporating the beauty of Chinese gardening. (Photo by Kang Lun'en)

In the pleasant mid-autumn season or on moonlit nights, Lin Erjia would invite friends to the garden to appreciate the bright moon and recite poetry, accompanied by the soothing sound of calm waves. That kind of sentimental experience would certainly add to one's admiration of this artfully designed garden, which agrees with the pursuit of romance and leisure that is deep at the core of the temperament of the island. Today, Shuzhuang Garden is open to visitors and has become not only the best known private garden of Kulangsu, but also one of the most important modern gardens in South China.

■ 八卦楼

鼓浪屿的地标建筑八卦楼（现鼓新路43号）始建于1907年，为林尔嘉的堂兄林鹤寿所建。八卦楼因顶部塔楼坐落于八边形平台上、八面开窗、圆顶有八条棱角而得名，也因其内部门道四通八达、形同八卦迷宫而得名。

八卦楼由当时的鼓浪屿救世医院院长郁约翰设计。通晓土木建筑工程的郁约翰为回报林鹤寿对救世医院的捐助，主动为林鹤寿设计他所希望的在鼓浪屿超越所有洋人别墅的最大别墅。八卦楼的设计以西方古典建筑风格为主，兼具本土风格，是一座以隔潮层为基础的四层楼砖混结构西式建筑，其建筑主体为一、二层楼，二层的楼顶为大露台，四周围砌女儿墙。三层是大露台中央的八边形平台，其顶部也是观景露台，周围砌女儿墙。四层为居中的圆塔，深红色的半球形塔顶成为八卦楼的标志。八卦楼具有典型的西方古典复兴建筑风格，在装饰和建造工艺上又具有厦门本土的地域特点。但是八卦楼命运多舛，林鹤寿因此巨大的工程破产，后又曾被日本人所占，在成为厦门市博物馆后近年变身为鼓浪屿风琴博物馆，对公众开放。当管风琴之音在八卦楼的穹顶下共鸣时，林鹤寿当年的心愿恐怕也算得偿了吧？

◎ 深红色的半球形塔顶是八卦楼的标志。（林乔森 摄）
The round tower on the top, adorned by the impressive crimson domed roof, is the symbol of Bagua Mansion. (Photo by Lin Qiaosen)

◎ 八卦楼内现有鼓浪屿风琴博物馆。（康伦恩 摄）

Kulangsu Organ Museum is now located in Bagua Mansion. (Photo by Kang Lun'en)

■ Bagua Mansion (Eight Trigrams Mansion)

Bagua Mansion (now at 43 Guxin Road) is a landmark building on Kulangsu, built in 1907 by Lin Heshou, a cousin of Lin Erjia. The mansion got its name because of its top tower, set on an octagonal base, with windows opening on eight sides and the eight angular cornices on the dome as well as because of its fully connected interior structure, which is exactly like an eight trigrams maze.

Bagua Mansion was designed by a Dutch American missionary named John Abraham Otte, who was then director of Hope Hospital. With a background of the civil engineering, John Otte designed the villa for Lin Heshou who had hoped to build the largest villa on Kulangsu, as a return for Lin's donation to the establishment of the hospital. The huge villa was primarily of Western Classical Revival Style, combined with local features. It was a four-storey building of brick and concrete structure based on the damp check. The first and second floors are the main structure of the building, and the roof of the second floor is a large terrace surrounded by parapets. The third floor is an octagonal platform in the middle of the terrace, which was also topped with a viewing terrace enclosed by parapets. The fourth floor is a round tower adorned by the impressive crimson domed roof which has now become the symbol of the mansion.

A typical example blending Western Classical Revival Architecture Style and local Amoy features in terms of the decoration and the craftsmanship, Bagua Mansion was not constructed smoothly. Lin Heshou went bankrupt because of the huge and costly project and the building was once occupied by Japanese. The building took on a new look when it became Xiamen Municipal Museum and a newer look quite recently in its new function as Kulangsu Organ Museum, one of Kulangsu's most important tourist attractions—both for its impressive collection of organs and for its stately and imposing architectural style.

◎ 黄家花园北楼。（康伦恩 摄）

The north building of Huang Family Villa. (Photo by Kang Lun'en)

■ 黄家花园

　　1919年，从印尼归国定居鼓浪屿的黄奕住，向林尔嘉购买了位于晃岩路原是洋行经理住宅的中德记，并将其改建为自住的黄家花园（现晃岩路33号）。黄家花园占地面积12,000平方米，建筑面积约4,500平方米，分为北、中、南三座住宅，呈中轴对称布局，其中主体建筑中楼向西后退20余米，形成东侧中心花园。

　　中楼于1921年由上海裕泰公司建造，高两层，呈现当时新潮的装饰艺术风格与南洋风格相结合的特征，造型洗练，却不显单调，富有现代感。整座建筑外立面全部采用洗石子饰面，施工技艺精湛。南北两座楼与中楼不同，装饰细部模仿西方古典主义建筑风格，屋顶老虎窗设计为带有巴洛克风格的装饰性山墙面。中心花园的设计也模仿了巴洛克风格。黄家花园位于日光岩脚下，俯瞰当时的"洋人球埔"，眼前无遮无挡，建成后被誉为"中国第一别墅"，后曾作为国宾馆，接待过不少中外政要。

■ Huang Family Villa

In 1919, Oei Tjoe, an overseas Chinese who returned from Indonesia to Kulangsu for permanent residence, bought from Lin Erjia the Tait Building at Huangyan Road which used to be residence for managers of a foreign bank. He rebuilt it into the Huang Family Villa (now at 33 Huangyan Road). Covering a land area of about 12,000m^2 and a floor space of some 4,500m^2, the villa consists of the north, central and south buildings, in a symmetrical central-axis layout. The main building in the middle was moved more than 20 meters westward to give space for the central garden on the east side.

The two-storey middle building was built by Shanghai Yutai Company in 1921, presenting trendy Art Deco Style blended with Southeast Asian elements, succinct, modern and varied. All the facades of the building were finished with washed pebbles, showcasing exquisite workmanship. Different from the middle building, the south and north buildings feature elaborate decorations imitating the Western Classical Revival Architectural Style, with ornate pediments of Baroco Style for the dormer on the roof. The same style was applied to the design of the central garden.

Sitting at the foot of Sunlight Rock and overlooking the former Foreigners' Football Field, the Huang Family Villa was praised as "The Best Villa in China" upon its completion. Later, it was used as a state guesthouse and received many state leaders from home and abroad.

◎ 气势恢宏的黄家花园。（林乔森 摄）
The magnificent Huang Family Villa. (Photo by Lin Qiaosen)

海天堂构（现福建路34号、36号、38号、40号和42号），是由菲律宾华侨黄秀烺和黄念忆共同于1920年到1930年间建成的宅园，由四座殖民地外廊风格的洋楼和最后建成的中西合璧风格的"中楼"组成，总占地面积6,500平方米。

海天堂构的中楼（现福建路38号）堪称鼓浪屿中西合璧的代表性建筑，整体风格呈现厦门装饰风格与"嘉庚风格"的折中。中楼的屋顶为岭南风格歇山屋顶，"出龟"门廊之上作重檐四坡攒尖小屋顶，屋顶飞檐作闽南传统风格的高高起翘。斗拱花篮，挑梁雀替，宝瓶栏杆，中式藻井，雕梁画栋，这些中式传统元素运用得淋漓尽致，使得海天堂构即使在豪华别墅林立的鼓浪屿，也称得上精彩绝伦。这种中西合璧的建筑，美国传教士毕腓力解读为华侨在海外受到欺凌，发家致富后在建筑上扬眉吐气，将中式风格压在西式建筑主体之上，是为"厌胜"。不过当年出洋的华侨，接受过西式的种种浸润，也算是开风气之先的一代人，中西合璧应该是他们独特的审美趋向。

◎ 海天堂构中楼。（杨戈 摄）
Central building of Hai Tian Tang Gou Mansion. (Photo by Yang Ge)

■ Hai Tian Tang Gou Mansion

Hai Tian Tang Gou Mansion (now at 34, 36, 38, 40 and 42 Fujian Road) was a private garden built from 1920s to 1930s by Huang Xiulang and Huang Nianyi, two overseas Chinese returning from the Philippines. Covering an area of 6,500m², it is a large building complex consisting of four Western-style houses of Veranda Colonial Style and a central building blending Chinese and Western architectural elements.

The central building of the mansion (now at 38 Fujian Road) is a fantastic example of both Western and Eastern styles on Kulangsu, compromising between Amoy Deco Style and "Tan Kah-kee Style". It features a hipped gable roof popular in South China, so named for the tiny double-eave pyramid hip over the protruding porch, with rising cornices of traditional South Fujian Style. Traditional Chinese elements found full expressions in brackets and braces with carvings of flowers and birds, as well as in balustrades, Chinese style caisson, and richly ornamented beams and rafters. All these raised Hai Tian Tang Gou Mansion into a league of its own among the luxurious villas on Kulangsu.

This union of Chinese and Western architectural styles was interpreted by American missionary Philip Wilson Pitcher to be an expression of "elation" of rich overseas Chinese after having been oppressed for too long in foreign lands and it was "symbolic" with Chinese style roof riding over the Western style main structure. This may have been but a superficial observation since it was only too natural for these open-minded overseas Chinese to be inclined to fusion of Chinese and Western elements, a unique aesthetic taste developed from their stay abroad and exposure to modern ideas.

◎ 中西合璧的海天堂构。（蔡松荣 摄）
Hai Tian Tang Gou Mansion with both Western and Eastern styles. (Photo by Cai Songrong)

■ 黄荣远堂

　　海天堂构对面的黄荣远堂（现福建路32号），原为1920年菲律宾华侨施光从由侨居地带回图纸建造而成，1931年转让给越南华侨黄仲训。黄仲训买下后，将其房地产公司"黄荣远堂"办事处总部从泉州路74号迁至该建筑。黄荣远堂中西合璧，主楼为三层殖民地式外廊建筑，入口两层高的半圆柱廊气势雄伟，圆形和半圆形的西式门窗装饰考究，三楼局部采用中式六角攒尖顶。主楼之外建有副楼。庭院运用了中国传统园林造景手法，在别墅正面中央挖出中轴对称、具有西方园林特征的双圆形嵌套形式的水池，与主体建筑轴线相对，在水池正中放置了太湖石。庭院西侧是人工堆成的中式云墙假山，假山上建有休憩观景的两亭一榭，庭院内花木扶疏。黄荣远堂风华未褪，坐在庭院里的假山上，可以看到隔邻的天主堂。这种感觉，似乎是那个年代小岛各种文化和谐共生的感觉。

◎ 黄荣远堂。（康伦恩 摄）
Huang Rongyuan Mansion. (Photo by Kang Lun'en)

◎ 黄荣远堂前有设计精巧的喷水池。（康伦恩 摄）
Ingeniously designed fountain in front of Huang Rongyuan
Mansion. (Photo by Kang Lun'en)

■ Huang Rongyuan Mansion

Opposite Hai Tian Tang Gou Mansion sits Huang Rongyuan Mansion (now at 32 Fujian Road),
first built in 1920 by Chinese Filipino Shi Guangcong based on design drawings he brought
back all the way from the Philippines. In 1931, Huang Zhongxun made the purchase and
moved the headquarters of his real estate firm "Huang Rongyuan" from its former location at
74 Quanzhou Road into this building.

The mansion integrated Chinese and Western architectural elements. The main building is
a three-storey one in Veranda Colonial Style, with the entrance of its front facade catching
the eye with a two-storey high semicircular protruding colonnade, and the finely decorated
circular and semicircular Western style windows and doors. Parts of the third floor were
designed with traditional Chinese hexagonal gable roof. There is a wing building and the
courtyard is an example of the traditional Chinese gardening and landscaping. The front of the
villa is centered by an axisymmetric double-circular nested fountain surrounded by Western
gardening. Against the axis of the main building, Taihu limestone rocks are placed in the center
of the fountain. In the west side of the garden there are artificial Chinese-style wavy cloud
walls and rockery, with two pavilions and a waterside kiosk for stopping and sight-seeing. Well-
preserved and in good repair today, Huang Rongyuan Mansion is still youthful, with blooming
flowers and green trees all around. Sitting on the rockery in the courtyard and admiring the
adjacent Catholic Church, one would be touched by the harmonious coexistence of different
cultures on the island back in those days.

■ 瞰青别墅和西林别墅

　　黄仲训还在日光岩上建有瞰青别墅（永春路73号）和西林别墅（永春路72号）。瞰青别墅始建于1916年，位于岩仔脚，砖木结构，"出龟"外廊，外廊的花瓣尖券、栏杆及屋顶形式体现出浓郁的东南亚殖民地建筑风格。瞰青别墅建成后，黄仲训在其东侧建"厚芳兰馆"，以纪念其父在越南的创业。西林别墅始建于1927年，位于日光岩西北侧，是一座建筑面积达2,100平方米的大型别墅。据说西林别墅是黄仲训从菲律宾带回设计图纸，请上海建筑队伍施工建设的。清水红砖与花岗岩条石墙角、半圆形"出龟"敞廊等相协调。别墅的细节十分耐看：变异的柯林斯柱头、檐口下的弧形斜撑、带装饰图案的栏杆。西林别墅傲视海天，如今隐于日光岩景区内，化身为"郑成功纪念馆"久矣。

◎ 西林别墅。（子健传媒 供图）
Xilin Villa. (Courtesy of Zijian Media)

■ Kanqing Villa and Xilin Villa

Huang Zhongxun also had Kanqing Villa (now at 73 Yongchun Road) and Xilin Villa (now at 72 Yongchun Road) built on Sunlight Rock. Construction of Kanqing Villa started in 1916 at Yanzijiao. This was a two-storey brick and wood structure with a protruding veranda, petal-shaped pointed arch, balustrades and roof which displays a rich sample of Southeast Asian colonial architecture. After the villa was completed, Huang Zhongxun built Houfanglan (Man of Virtue) Memorial in memory of his father's enterprising career in Vietnam. Xilin Villa started construction in 1927 to the northwest of Sunlight Rock and was a grand villa covering a floor space of 2,100m². It was said that Huang Zhongxun brought back design drawings from the Philippines and had construction teams brought in from Shanghai for the project. The fairfaced red-brick wall and granite cornerstone went naturally with the protruding semicircular open-air veranda. Every detail was handled with care, such as a variation of the Corinthian order, curved brace under eaves, and balustrades with decorative designs. Enjoying a panoramic view of the sea, Xilin Villa is used now as Koxinga Memorial.

■ **李传别别墅**

　　黄荣远堂对面的李传别别墅（现福建路44号），约建于20世纪20年代，1935年被印尼华侨茶商李传别买下，从两层扩建为三层，并建附楼。该别墅红砖墙体为清水和密缝两种砌法，墙角为闽南传统的出砖入石，拱券十字栏杆，厦门装饰风格鲜明。李传别别墅附近的许家园（现鹿礁路38号）、菲侨别墅（现福建路26号、28号、30号）、美园（现鹿礁路7号）和海滨旅社（现鹿礁路2号）都是典型的厦门装饰风格别墅，至今韵味犹存。

■ Li Chuanbie Villa

Opposite Huang Rongyuan Mansion is Li Chuanbie Villa (now at 44 Fujian Road) built in the 1920s. In 1935, it was purchased by Li Chuanbie, an overseas Chinese tea merchant from Indonesia, and expanded from two storeys to three together with the addition of a wing. The red brick wall of the villa was made by using fairfaced and close-joints bricklaying methods. The corner was a mixture of brick and stone, a traditional South Fujian Style of building stone blocks into a brick wall. The arched cross railings are in distinct Amoy Deco Style. This style is found in quite a few neighboring mansions and villas, such as Xu Family Mansion (now at 38 Lujiao Road), Philippine Overseas Chinese Villa (now at 26, 28 and 30 Fujian Road), Meiyuan Garden (now at 7 Lujiao Road) and Seaside Hotel (now at 2 Lujiao Road). They are all tourist attractions today.

◎ 李传别别墅。（子健传媒 供图）
Li Chuanbie Villa. (Courtesy of Zijian Media)

■ 闽南圣教书局

福建路上还有一幢看起来颇为普通的红砖别墅，为闽南圣教书局旧址（现福建路43号）。1932年，由教会人士捐献地皮和经费，在福建路、龙头路、晃岩路的交叉路口建起了这幢三层洋楼，清水红砖，平屋顶，建筑在街道拐角处作切角处理。这幢小楼曾是中国基督教书籍发行中心之一，还委托印刷《圣经教义》等书籍，其中仅用白话字印刷的书籍就有100多种。

■ Former Bookstore of South Fukien Religious Tract Society

On Fujian Road there is another plain looking but worthy red-brick villa. It is the former Bookstore of South Fukien Religious Tract Society (now at 43 Fujian Road). In 1932, church members donated land and funds to build this three-storey Western style building at the intersection of Fujian Road, Longtou Road and Huangyan Road. A fair faced red-brick and flat-roof structure located on a street corner, the building used to be a distribution center of Christian publications in China.

The Christian bookstore also entrusted the task of printing *Biblical Doctrines* and other books to a local printery. More than 100 kinds of POJ books were printed.

◎ 闽南圣教书局。（康伦恩 摄）
Bookstore of South Fukien Religious Tract Society. (Photo by Kang Lun'en)

◎ 番婆楼。（林乔森 摄）
Fanpo Mansion. (Photo by Lin Qiaosen)

■ 番婆楼

　　拥有鼓浪屿最高门楼的番婆楼（现安海路36号），建于20世纪20年代，为菲律宾华侨许经权所建。番婆楼是一座大型殖民地外廊式别墅建筑，带有浓郁的厦门装饰风格特征。番婆楼有主楼与附楼，主楼高两层，中轴对称，文艺复兴风格的外廊、清水红砖砌筑、砖拱券与建筑的转角红砖间隔嵌入石块，整体效果绚丽多彩。建筑外立面的浮雕装饰题材多样，中西文化题材皆有。庭院的设计也是中西合璧，有假山，有中式如意漏窗，铁门上刻有中式"福"字。番婆楼一直由许经权后人居住，维护良好。可惜近年易主，被改造得面目全非。

■ Fanpo Mansion

Fanpo Mansion (now at 36 Anhai Road) was known for the highest archway on Kulangsu built in 1927 by Xu Jingquan, an overseas Chinese in the Philippines. It is a villa in Veranda Colonial Style, tinted with rich Amoy Deco elements. A complex consisting of a main house and a wing, Fanpo Mansion has its two-storey main building in a central-axis symmetrical layout, with Renaissance styled verandas, and fair faced red brick masonry, alternating with white stones to produce a brilliant use of color. The facade of the building was decorated with a diverse range of Chinese and Western themes. The courtyard was also designed by combining Chinese elements, such as rockery, lattice windows and the iron gate engraved with the Chinese character "福" (Blessings). The house was lived in by descendants of Xu Jingquan and well maintained, but has changed a lot in recent years with different owners.

■ 容谷别墅

　　升旗山麓的容谷别墅（现旗山路1号），是菲律宾木材大王李清泉所建、赠予夫人颜漱的别墅。别墅修建于1926年，由旅美中国建筑师设计督造，依山势而布局，有主楼与附楼。主楼三层，建筑平面中轴对称，白色门廊通高两层，建筑主体清水红砖，外廊宽阔，屋内楼梯地板均使用上好的楠木。庭院曲径环绕，由彩色卵石铺砌成各种西式图案，建有喷水池，西侧高地上建有一座西式六角亭，可赏厦鼓绝佳风景。容谷别墅虽经几次易主，但楼前与别墅同龄的南洋松生机不减，已高出别墅主楼。

◎ 容谷别墅。（康伦恩 摄）
Banyan Valley Villa. (Photo by Kang Lun'en)

◎ 容谷内绿树掩映。（康伦恩 摄）
Banyan Valley Villa is framed by green trees. (Photo by Kang Lun'en)

■ Banyan Valley Villa

Banyan Valley Villa (now at 1 Qishan Road) at the foot of Flag-Raising Hill was a villa built by Li Qingquan, an overseas Chinese timber tycoon in the Philippines, as a gift for his wife Yan Shu. Built in 1926 and consisting of a main building and attached secondary buildings, the villa was designed and constructed by overseas Chinese architects from the United States by taking advantage of the natural terrain. There are three floors in the main building, which is in a central-axis symmetrical layout. The white porch is two storeys high and the main building is a fairfaced red brick structure, with a spacious veranda, timber stairs and floors made of high quality Nanmu. The garden was designed with utmost care, with a fountain surrounded by winding paths paved with colored pebbles in various patterns. On the slope to its west lies a Western style hexagonal pavilion, offering a panoramic view of Amoy and Kulangsu. Although the villa has been through several owners, the southern pine in front of the building, planted at the same time as the house was constructed, has outgrown the main building and is still full of life and as youthful as it used to be.

■ 杨家园

　　笔架山东侧的杨家园（现鼓新路27号、29号、31号，安海路4号），由菲律宾华侨杨忠权、杨知母、杨启泰兴建。1913年前后，杨氏兄弟向英国差会购得一栋旧房，请工匠拆旧建新。到20世纪30年代，建成四座洋楼，名为"杨家园"。四座洋楼均属厦门装饰风格，采用钢筋混凝土柱梁结构，每座建筑都在正面设置外廊。这几座建筑皆采用石墙基，柱、梁、门窗套以及院墙大门都采用洗石子（也有少量磨石子）仿石装饰，与烟炙红砖砌筑的清水砖墙搭配，凸显出质感和色彩对比。具体的装饰偏向于模仿西方巴洛克风格，也有仿西方古典主义的柱头和装饰艺术风格的局部装饰。整座杨家园是华侨所建的厦门装饰风格建筑的代表作品。还值得一提的是，杨家园的供水设施先进实用，为当时的鼓浪屿之最。

◎ 杨家园。（子健传媒 供图）
Yang Family Mansion. (Courtesy of Zijian Media)

◎ 杨家园内繁花似锦。（子健传媒 供图）

Plants are in full bloom at Yang Family Mansion. (Courtesy of Zijian Media)

■ Yang Family Mansion

Yang Family Mansion, located in the east side of Bijia Hill (now at 27, 29, 31 Guxin Road and 4 Anhai Road), was built by Yang Zhongquan, Yang Zhimu and Yang Qitai, brothers of an overseas Chinese family in the Philippines. They purchased an old house from British Missionary Society and had craftsmen renovate it around 1913. By the 1930s, the construction of a complex of four Western-style houses was completed and given the name "Yang Family Mansion". Featuring the Amoy Deco Style, all four buildings are reinforced concrete column-beam structure with protruding verandas in the front and stone wall foundations. The columns, beams, door frames and windows as well as gates are decorated with washed pebbles (and a few terrazzos), which went with fairfaced smoke red bricks to produce a contrast in color and texture. The details of the decoration imitated the Western Baroque Style, while some pillar capitals followed the Western Classical Revival Style and others were of the Art Deco Style.

A typical example of the Amoy Deco Style built by overseas Chinese, Yang Family Mansion also boasted convenient and state-of-the-art water supply facilities of the time on Kulangsu.

笔山上的春草堂（现笔山路17号）建于1933年，也是厦门装饰风格突出的别墅。它是从事建筑行业、白手起家创办了厦门最大的建筑公司并组织创立了"厦门市建筑总工会"的许春草为自己设计建造的住宅。两层高的春草堂位于笔架山西北制高点，风光无限。建筑平面中轴对称，主体为矩形，正面设三开间柱廊，正中开间为半圆形平面的"出龟"，建筑转角部分设洗石子装饰仿花岗岩石块立柱，后面衬清水红砖立柱。红砖和花岗岩质感和谐，毫不突兀，颇具闽南乡土风格。

■ Chuncao Villa

Built in 1933, Chuncao Villa is located today at 17 Bishan Road and is also a house typical of the Amoy Deco Style. It was designed and built by Xu Chuncao, a building contractor of one of the most famous construction companies in Xiamen at the time, who started from nothing and founded the "General Construction Union in Xiamen". Located at the highest point in the northwest of Bijia Hill, the two-storey building offers stunning views. Laid out around a central axis, the central structure is rectangular in shape. There is a three-bay colonnade at the front of the villa, with the middle area protruding in a semicircle. The corner of the building was decorated with granitic plaster and imitation granite stone pillars set against fairfaced red brick columns at the back. The red brick complements the granite in texture which reflects the local style in South Fujian.

◎ 春草堂。（康伦恩 摄）
Chuncao Villa. (Photo by Kang Lun'en)

■ 林屋

　　林屋（现泉州路82号），原址为1880年建成的教会"杜嘉德纪念堂"。因白蚁蛀毁而被教会长老林振勋买下，并让其留学美国麻省理工学院的次子（设计了厦门自来水公司的林全诚）设计成自家的别墅。林屋的蒙萨屋顶波折起伏，外廊的栏杆因长得像咧嘴模样，被戏称为"奸笑墙"。这座法式风格的别墅，衬着花园内高大的柠檬桉，个性而典雅。

◎ 林屋。（子健传媒 供图）
Lin's House. (Courtesy of Zijian Media)

■ Lin's House

Lin's House at 82 Quanzhou Road was built on the former site of the church's "Cartairs Douglas Memorial", which was completed in 1880 but destroyed by termites. The dilapidated house was then bought by Lin Zhenxun, chairman of the church, who asked his second son Lin Quancheng, who studied at Massachusetts Institute of Technology and had designed Amoy Water Supply Company, to design his own villa. The mansard roof, a four-sided gambrel-style hip roof, is undulating and the railings on the outer veranda have been nicknamed the "wall of sly laughter" for their grinning appearance. This French-style villa, set against tall lemon eucalyptus in the garden, is unique and elegant.

■ 金瓜楼

在鼓浪屿上远远就能看到其"金瓜"屋顶的黄赐敏别墅（现泉州路99号），因两个"金瓜"穹顶又名"金瓜楼"。该别墅建于1922年，为旅菲华侨黄赐敏所有。"金瓜楼"也是厦门装饰风格中中西合璧的建筑代表。其建筑中轴对称，平面采用三开间布局，建筑侧立面采用清水红砖墙，只有外廊、壁柱、过梁处以白色洗石子面层装饰。柱廊的柱头、柱杆、挂落、檐口，以及壁柱、墙面都饰以精致的花卉禽鸟主题的灰塑。穹顶八棱饰春草飞卷，生动细腻。

■ Huang Cimin Villa

On Kulangsu, another easily identifiable building is Huang Cimin Villa (now at 99 Quanzhou Road) for its two eye-catching "Golden Pumpkin" domes. Built in 1922 and owned by Huang Cimin, an overseas Chinese in the Philippines, the villa was otherwise called "Golden Pumpkin Villa" because of the two eight-edged pyramid domes in the shape of a pumpkin. Another remarkable example of the Amoy Deco Style integrating Chinese and Western elements, the building is a three-bay structure symmetrical around a central axis. Fairfaced red brick wall was used for the side facade and white pebble decorations adorned the veranda, pilasters and architraves. The cap, poles, hangings and cornice of the colonnades as well as pilasters and walls were finely carved with plaster patterns of flowers and birds and the eight-edged pyramid domes were vividly designed with delicate lines.

◎ 金瓜楼拥有两个标志性的穹顶。（林乔森 摄）
Golden Pumpkin Villa has two symbolic domes. (Photo by Lin Qiaosen)

◎ 黄赐敏别墅。（康伦恩 摄）
Huang Cimin Villa. (Photo by Kang Lun'en)

鼓浪屿还有许多归国华侨兴建的洋楼。一个世纪过去，它们仍在巷弄与山间伫立。过去它们是发家致富后的归国华侨叶落归根，想要寻找理想家园的寄托，现在则是我们怀想那个繁华时代的凭借。人去楼空也好，改作他途也好，这些洋楼、别墅到底也是一种见证，见证过一座岛屿的风流过往。

　　万国建筑，是鼓浪屿之歌里最动人的音符，是流动的盛宴，是漫步岛屿时时可遇见的风景。它们无法抵御时间的流逝，但时间也是它们最好的标注。哪怕人去楼空，朝代更迭，那些廊柱窗棂，那些飞檐雕花，依然是每一个传奇故事里不曾或缺的注脚。它承接，起兴，是一首永恒的诗。

◎ 重建后的林氏府。（康伦恩 摄）
Lin's House after renovation. (Photo by Kang Lun'en)

◎ 许家园。（杨戈 摄）
Xu Family Mansion. (Photo by Yang Ge)

There are many other mansions and villas on Kulangsu built by returned overseas Chinese that are still standing amid back streets and hills even a hundred years have passed. What used to be expressions of returned overseas Chinese for a sweet home in their own motherland after they had made a fortune on foreign lands, has become something we rely on today as testament of that golden era. The houses may be deserted or used for other purposes, but still they witness the beautiful changes on Kulangsu.

The diverse architectural styles are the most touching notes in the Song of Kulangsu. They are a feast for the eyes and sights one may encounter while strolling on the island. They can't resist the passage of time, but instead are testimony of the time that has passed. Despite the deserted buildings and the change of times, those columns and window lattices as well as cornices and carvings are details indispensable in every tale told from one generation to the next.

外来宗教——左手医疗，右手教育

在厦门成为《南京条约》签署后首批开放的口岸之一前，鼓浪屿就成了基督教传教士的大本营。1842年2月，美国归正教会牧师雅裨理搭乘英国军舰抵达鼓浪屿，雅裨理因此成为近代基督教进入福建传教的第一人，而厦门也成为继广州之后，基督教进入中国的第二个城市。美国归正教会、伦敦差会、大英长老会联合成立了英美"三公会"，三公会先以鼓浪屿为落脚点，再到厦门建教堂、办识字班、开诊所，以此开启传教工作。

随着鸦片战争的战舰，传教士们纷至沓来。

天主教也循着曾经在厦门留下的足迹，重回旧地。1842年，多明我会传教士林方济到鼓浪屿宣教，他是鸦片战争后最早进入厦门的天主教宣教士。

1843年11月2日，厦门正式开埠。英军舰长纪里布成为首任英国驻厦门领事，几个月以后，由阿礼国接任。前期到达鼓浪屿的传教士们都得到了英军的优待。

基督教是公共地界时期鼓浪屿最大的教派势力。最早来到鼓浪屿的是基督教的美国归正教会，接着是英国伦敦差会和长老会，美国安息日会、基督教青年会、基督教女青年会也先后踏足。基督教把鼓浪屿当作在闽南传播福音的门户与根据地，再沿着九龙江向闽南各地及台湾扩展，"（1911年）这些差会设置了9个中心，即永春、惠安、泉州、同安、漳州、厦门、漳浦、小溪和汀州。"

◎ 20世纪30年代英国传教士合影。（白桦 供图）

Missionaries from Britain in the 1930s. (Courtesy of Bai Hua)

Foreign Religions: Spreading the Gospel Through Medicine and Education

Even before Amoy was opened as one of the first commercial ports with the *Treaty of Nanking (Nanjing)*, Kulangsu was already a stronghold for Christian missionaries. In February 1842, David Abeel, a missionary of the American Reformed Church, arrived at Kulangsu by a British warship to make himself the first evangelist to come to Fujian in modern times. As a result, Amoy became the second Chinese city exposed to Christianity after Guangzhou. Later, the American Reformed Church, London Missionary Society and British Presbyterian Church co-founded the Three Societies which started in Kulangsu before they expanded to spread the Gospel in Amoy by building churches, schools and medical clinics.

More missionaries came with the warships of the Opium War.

Catholics also returned following the footsteps of those who left Amoy. In 1842, François da Sylvax, a missionary of Catholic Ordo Dominicanorum, arrived on Kulangsu. François da Sylvax was the first Catholic missionary to come to Amoy after the Opium War.

When Amoy was forced to open as a commercial port on November 2, 1843, Captain Henry Gribble was appointed as the first British Consul to Amoy and Sir Rutherford Alcock took over a few months later. Missionaries who arrived at Kulangsu in early times were given preferential treatment by the British army.

Christianity was the most influential religion on Kulangsu during the settlement period. The first religion to come to Kulangsu was the American Reformed Church, followed by the London Missionary Society, British Presbyterian Church, American Sabbath Church, the Young Men's Christian Association (YMCA) and the Young Women's Christian Association. Christianity took Kulangsu as the gateway and base to spread the Gospel in South Fujian, and then expanded to all adjacent areas along the Jiulongjiang River and as far as Taiwan. "1911 saw these churches set up nine branches in places like Yongchun, Hui'an, Quanzhou, Tong'an, Zhangzhou, Amoy, Zhangpu, Xiaoxi and Tingzhou."

◎ 1892年美国归正教牧师与田尾女学堂学生
合影。（白桦 供图）
Missionaries of American Reformed Church with students of Tianwei Girls' School, 1892.
(Courtesy of Bai Hua)

教育与医疗，既是教会不可或缺的深入当地的途径，也使鼓浪屿的居民率先得到现代医疗的庇护，以及可以较早接受先进的教育：那些在教会受教育的孩子，有的是穷苦出身，本是上不起学的；有的则在这里开了眼界——林语堂便在鼓浪屿从教会小学到寻源中学，接受了7年标准的西方式教育，鼓浪屿的西式文化令年少的他倍感新鲜，他甚至在《八十自述》中写到当年他在教会中学所受到的影响。著名诗人舒婷的父亲出生在鼓浪屿，毕业于岛上教会所办的英华男中，母亲则毕业于同是教会所办的毓德女中。教育所带来的改变同样被历史深深记取。

◎ 1949年美华中学师生。（白桦 供图）

Teachers and students of Meihua (American-Chinese) High School, 1949. (Courtesy of Bai Hua)

　　有人评价说："正是这些早期的教会家庭和他们由教会学校培养出来的子女，支撑起鼓浪屿的别有天地。他们是第一群从社会底层开眼看世界的中国人。"

　　而那些埋骨异乡的传教士，曾埋葬在岛屿上"大宫口"的洋人墓地内（也称"番仔墓"）和鸡母山麓的"基督教会墓园"。"番仔墓"因建设鼓浪屿音乐厅而消散于历史尘烟中，基督教会墓园保存完好，连传教士的墓碑文字都清晰可见，有一些传教士早夭的孩子、新婚便去世的妻子也埋葬于此，还有一些著名的华人牧师和教徒，如"中国切音字第一人"卢戆章，亦长眠于此。

◎ 基督教会墓园。（子健传媒 供图）
Cemetery of Christian Church. (Courtesy of Zijian Media)

◎ 20世纪20年代鼓浪屿怀德幼稚园的老师和孩子。（白桦 供图）

A teacher and her students at Huaide Kindergarten, Kulangsu, in the 1920s. (Courtesy of Bai Hua)

Education and medicine had been considered by the church to be the most effective means for the spreading of its belief. They were not only indispensable for the church to take root on Kulangsu, but also beneficial to local residents, including children from poor families, for they could gain access to modern education and modern medical care at an earlier time. Many children were initially exposed to foreign religion here, such as Lin Yutang. He received seven years of modern education from a church-run primary school and Xunyuan High School on Kulangsu, which inspired him and deeply impressed him. The influence was so unforgettable that he gave an account of his time there in his autobiography *Memories at Eighty*. The famous poet Shu Ting's father was born on Kulangsu and graduated from church-run Anglo-Chinese (Yinghua) Boys' School while her mother was a graduate from Loktek Girls' School, another church-run high school. These great changes brought about by Western education have been recorded in history.

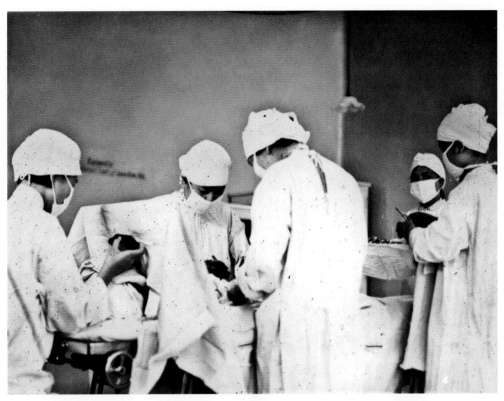

◎ 救世医院医生做手术。（白桦 供图）
Doctors of the Hope Hospital were performing an operation. (Courtesy of Bai Hua)

This is summarized by the following comments: "It was these early church families and their children nurtured by church schools that gave support to Kulangsu as a unique land. They were the first group of ordinary Chinese people to open their eyes to the outside world from the bottom of society."

Foreign missionaries who died here far away from home were once buried on the island's "Dagongkou" Cemetery (also known as "Fanzi Tombs"), reserved for foreigners and the "Cemetery of Christian Church" at the foot of Jimu Hill. The former is no longer there and on the site is now Kulangsu Music Hall, while the latter remains intact, with legible tombstone inscriptions. Lying here are also children of some missionaries who died young, deceased newly-wed wives of missionaries, as well as famous Chinese pastors and Christians, including Lu Zhuangzhang, "China's pioneer of the Pinyin system".

教会的医疗救治

西洋医术进入中国，基督教起了重要的启迪和推动作用。

已经在鼓浪屿传教的美国归正教会的雅裨理深感现代医疗的重要，他给好朋友、正在新加坡的甘明医生写信求援。甘明随即来到鼓浪屿。1842年6月7日，雅裨理和甘明在鼓浪屿开设了一个小型的诊所，诊所就设在雅裨理当时租来的靠海的民房中，这间小平房便是厦门的第一家西医诊所。后来该诊所迁往厦门。

Church Provided Medical Care

The introduction of Western medicine to China owes a lot to Christianity.

David Abeel was a missionary of the American Reformed Church who had been preaching on Kulangsu. Feeling strongly about the importance of modern medicine, he wrote to his close friend Doctor William Henry Cumming in Singapore, who came immediately at his request. On June 7, 1842, Abeel and Cumming opened a clinic on Kulangsu in a house they rented by the sea, which was the first Western medicine clinic in the Amoy area. Later on, the clinic was relocated to Amoy.

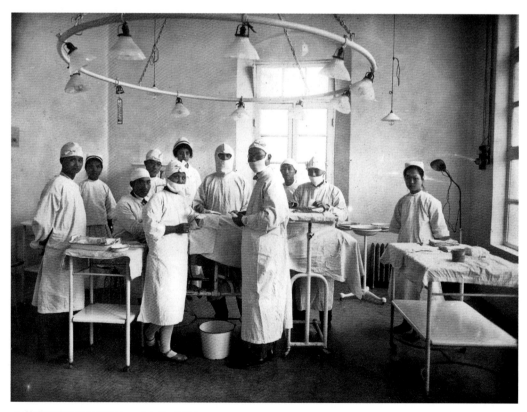

◎ 救世医院的医生和护士。（白桦 供图）
Doctors and nurses with Hope Hospital. (Courtesy of Bai Hua)

1872年到1893年间，美国人在鼓浪屿上后来建造领事馆的地方，办了一家"海上医院"，专为外国水手服务。

但基督教会在鼓浪屿真正的医疗工作始于救世医院（现鼓新路80号）。1898年，归正教会将救世男女医院总院由平和小溪移至鼓浪屿河仔下，这是厦门第一所西医医院。救世医院分设"救世男医馆"和"救世女医馆"，经费来自民间和教会捐助，曾接受当时荷兰女王的捐款，因此医院旗杆上曾挂荷兰王国三色国旗。救世医院是鼓浪屿第一座医院，也曾是闽南最大的综合性医院。

◎ 当年的救世女医馆。（陈亚元 供图）
Hope & Wilhelmina Hospital in the old days. (Courtesy of Chen Yayuan)

Between 1872 and 1893, a Marine Hospital was set up by the American to serve foreign sailors on the site where the American Consulate would be established later.

However, regular Western medical care offered by the Christian church started from Hope Hospital (now at 80 Guxin Road), the first Western medicine hospital in Amoy. In 1898, missionaries of the Reformed Church moved the headquarters of the general Hope Hospital in Xiaoxi Town to a new site in Hezixia, which was subdivided into departments for male and female patients. The hospital was funded by donations from the church and the community, including a donation from Dutch Queen Wilhelmina, so the hospital was also known as "Hope & Wilhelmina Hospital" and on the flagpole of the hospital was once the tricolor flag of the Kingdom of the Netherlands. Hope Hospital was the first hospital on Kulangsu and the biggest general hospital in South Fujian.

郁约翰是救世医院第一任院长，其后的院长有木英雄、夏礼文及华人医师陈五爵等。医院所有医生，都从医学院毕业，医院较为正规，且医护人员具备一定的素质。救世医院设有内科、外科、产科、眼耳鼻科。

1932年，救世医院从美国购进X光机，医院开始有较大型的设备。该院开始设病床，收治内科、外科、妇产科、眼耳鼻科病人和实施外科手术。救世医院有手术室2间，问诊室6间，特别病房30间，普通病房9间，还有实验室、X光室、药房等。20世纪30年代，厦门救世医院率先开展常规血液检查和胸部透视。救世医院的外科主任陈荣殿博士当时已能开展胃部分切除术。

1900年，美国归正教会在其所办的救世医院内还创办了厦门救世医院医学专门学校，校长由医院的历任院长兼任，医院各科医生担任教学，学制5年。从1900年至1932年，学校培养了6届毕业生，共46人。这些毕业生后来都成为闽南医界翘楚，救死扶伤无数。

1926年，救世医院附设护士学校，同时兼办助产士学校，培养护理人员。这是闽南地区第一所护士学校。护士学校共招生22届，毕业生160人。

救世医院的历史也正是19世纪末至20世纪初鼓浪屿西方医疗机构创办、发展的历史。它的建立为厦门乃至福建及东南亚带来了现代意义上的医学技术、医疗设备和医疗服务。

◎ 郁约翰和他的中国学生。（陈亚元 供图）
Dr. Otte with his Chinese students. (Courtesy of Chen Yayuan)

◎ 救世医院附设护士学校旧址。（林乔森 摄）

Former Attached Nurses' School to Hope Hospital. (Photo by Lin Qiaosen)

John Abraham Otte was the first president of Hope Hospital and his successors were also missionary doctors, including Clarence H. Holleman and Chinese doctor Chen Wujue. With certified doctors and nurses, the hospital was well-organized, divided into departments of internal medicine, surgery, obstetrics, ophthalmology, otology and otorhinolaryngology.

In 1932, the hospital purchased X-ray machines from the United States and was better equipped, with ward beds ready for the treatment of patients. There were internal medicine surgery, obstetrics and gynecology, ophthalmology, otology and otorhinolaryngology. There were two operation rooms, six examination rooms, thirty special wards, nine general wards, one laboratory, one X-ray room, and one pharmacy. Surgical operations were conducted. In the 1930s, the hospital began to carry out routine blood tests and chest fluoroscopy, and its chief of surgery Dr. Chen Rongdian was then able to perform a partial gastrectomy.

In 1900, the American Reformed Church established an attached medical school on the premises of Hope Hospital, and all presidency was held concurrently by previous directors of the hospital. Five-year courses were taught by doctors from all hospital departments. From 1900 to 1932, a total of 46 people graduated from the school, who all later became key figures in medical circles in South Fujian and treated numerous patients.

In 1926, an attached nurses' school was set up in the hospital, along with a midwifery school, which was the earliest nurses' school in South Fujian. A total of 160 students graduated from there across 22 years.

The history of the hospital was one of the establishment and development of Western medical institutions on Kulangsu from the late 19th to the early 20th centuries. Its establishment had brought to Amoy, Fujian and even Southeast Asia modern medical technology, equipment and services.

"本院设立宗旨在传播救恩，医治疾病，服务社会，健康人群，并促成医学之进步，指导卫生之常识。"1910年4月6日，因诊治一个患上肺炎型鼠疫的青年病人，郁约翰染上鼠疫，英年早逝。他要求安葬在鼓浪屿。他的学生黄大辟等人在医院门前造塔镌碑以纪其功："郁约翰牧师美国人也，医学博士。学称厥名，志宏厥名，志弘厥学。侨厦敷教施诊，精心毅力，廿载靡濡。手创医院三，授徒成业二十余辈，功效聿著，愿力弥宏。以身殉志，生不遗力，殁不归骨，卒践誓言，葬于兹丘。追念功德，表石以记。石可泐，骨可朽，先生功德不可没。诸学生全泐石。"碑文分别用英、荷、拉丁和闽南白话文四种文字镌刻，镶嵌在四个正立面。

救世医院现已改建成故宫鼓浪屿外国文物馆。院内老树扶疏，院外海岸绵延，长眠异国的郁约翰以及救世医院，无疑是小岛的另一段编年史。

◎ 救世医院旧址。（林乔森 摄）
Former Hope Hospital. (Photo by Lin Qiaosen)

◎ 救世医院护士学校学生毕业照。（白桦 供图）
Graduate photo of Attached Nurses' School to Hope Hospital. (Courtesy of Bai Hua)

As stated in the mission of the hospital proposed by John Abraham Otte: "Our purpose is to spread hope of life and cure diseases so as to better serve the community and promote health. Efforts will be made to contribute to the progress of medicine and enhance common knowledge about public health." And John himself walked the walk. On April 6, 1910, during a home visit to a young patient suffering from the pneumonic plague, John caught the plague and died young. He was buried on Kulangsu at his request. His student Huang Dapi and others built a monument in front of the hospital to pay tribute to his contributions and the inscriptions read: "Here lies John Abraham Otte, an American, MD and a man with great aspirations. He devoted himself to curing the wounded, rescuing the dying, and passing his knowledge to his students. He established three hospitals and taught with all his heart for more than 20 years, developing excellent medical graduates. He spared no efforts to help others and died to save others on a foreign land. He was buried here according to his will. In memory of his merits and virtues, this monument was built. The stone may be worn away and his bone may decay, but his spirit will never die. Love from all his students." Written in four languages, English, Dutch, Latin and South Fujian POJ, the inscriptions were engraved on the four facades of the monument.

Hope Hospital has now become Kulangsu Gallery of Foreign Artifacts from the Palace Museum Collection. The old trees in the hospital and the stretching coastline outside, together with Hope Hospital and John Abraham Otte who lied here in a foreign land, constitute by themselves another important part of the island's history.

除了救世医院，鼓浪屿的医疗近代化还有一所医院不可忽视。1925年曾在鼓浪屿救世医院供职、1924年成为美国领事馆主治医官、时任鼓浪屿工部局董事长的美国归正教会医生锡鸿恩在其住所开设了"锡鸿恩诊所"（现鼓新路44号）。诊所后来获得了"美国公共卫生署"的资金赞助，并有黄大辟、黄宜甫、林遵行等中国籍医生参与共事、共同经营，因此更名为"宏宁医院"。兴建稍晚的现鼓新路46号建筑也成为宏宁医院用房。

1927年，锡鸿恩离开鼓浪屿后，宏宁医院业绩下滑，于1933年并入救世医院。其后，由宏宁医院培养出来的一批本土医生，由林遵行医师提议，于1931年10月联合商人黄钦书、杨忠懿、许经权、陈荣芳等资方代表，共同筹组"私立鼓浪屿医院"，借宏宁医院原址开业。1938年厦门沦陷后，大批难民避难鼓浪屿，私立鼓浪屿医院也一度成为收容难民的地方。二战结束后，这里成为联合国国际救济总署及民国时期行政院善后救济总署在鼓浪屿指定的唯一一家进行善后医疗救济的医院。

私立鼓浪屿医院沉寂多年，洋楼风姿仍存，善后救济总署"CNRRA"的标志和岁月的痕迹一起镌刻在建筑的外墙上。屋里当年被磨损的花砖、建筑的格局都是一所医院的佐证。因为医院的建筑在鼓新路的转角处，红砖石墙，雕花窗棂，有人形容这里是"鼓浪屿最美的转角"。也许在特殊的战争年代，能给人带来希望的所在才是美好的所在吧。

◎ 私立鼓浪屿医院产科部婴孩摄影纪念。（白桦 供图）
Staff from obstetrics department of Private Kulangsu Hospital with new-born babies. (Courtesy of Bai Hua)

◎ 私立鼓浪屿医院旧址。（子健传媒 供图）
Former Private Kulangsu Hospital. (Courtesy of Zijian Media)

Modern medicine on Kulangsu can also be credited to another missionary doctor and his hospital. In 1925, Edward J. Strick, who worked at Hope Hospital and became the chief doctor of the Consulate General of the US in 1924, opened "Edward J. Strick Clinic" at his residence (now at 44 Guxin Road) when he was also acting as the board chairman of the Kulangsu Municipal Council. Later, the clinic received funds from the Public Health Service of the US and invited Chinese doctors such as Huang Dapi, Huang Yifu and Lin Zunxing for joint operation, and the hospital was renamed "Hongning Hospital". The building at 46 Guxin Road was built later and used by the hospital.

In 1927, Edward J. Strick left Kulangsu and Hongning Hospital suffered from a decline in business, and eventually merged with Hope Hospital in 1933. Initiated by Lin Zunxing, local doctors fostered by Hongning Hospital cooperated with representatives of employers Huang Qinshu, Yang Zhongyi, Xu Jingquan and Chen Rongfang in October 1931 to open a hospital named "Private Kulangsu Hospital" which was located at the original site of Hongning Hospital. After Amoy was occupied by the Japanese in 1938, a large number of refugees came to Kulangsu and the hospital became a shelter for refugees. After the war, Private Kulangsu Hospital was the only one on Kulangsu offering rehabilitation and medical relief designated by the China National Relief and Rehabilitation Administration (CNRRA) of the Republic of China under an agreement with the United Nations Relief and Rehabilitation Administration (UNRRA).

The Private Kulangsu Hospital was shut down long ago but the building remains intact today together with the weather-beaten logo of "CNRRA" engraved in the outer wall. The wear and tear and layout of the building all indicate that this place used to be a hospital. It happens that the red-brick, stone walled building with carved windows sits at the corner of Guxin Road and has therefore been described as "the prettiest corner on Kulangsu". It is, particularly during times of war, when the hospital represented life and hope.

教会所办的女学和小学

　　从19世纪50年代到公共地界时期，传教士在鼓浪屿上兴办起各种各样的学校：幼儿园、小学、中学、师范、专门的医学校、职业学校、神学院，还有针对妇女的妇学、难童学校……有走读的，有寄宿的；有男学，有女学。教会学校加上中国人办的私立学校、公办学校，使鼓浪屿这个小岛成了闽南一带学校最多、最密集的地方。甚至在1917年，美国归正教会还派来儿童专家卫升平在鼓浪屿设立美归正教会教育部，领导归正教在闽南等地创办的教会学校。

　　早期的教会学校规模较小，学生人数也少，多的不过十几人、二十人，少的也就寥寥数人。学校通常附设在教堂内或传教士的住宅内，主要教学识字和宗教教育，推广闽南白话字，类似启蒙教育。

　　第二次鸦片战争后，教会发展迅猛，西洋的教育也因之发展起来。加上中国的洋务运动倡办新式学堂，西洋的教育制度给原本的八股科举制度带来了一定的冲击和影响，就读教会学校的学生逐渐增多。这一阶段，鼓浪屿的小学教育开始普遍发展起来，有的学校还男女学生并收。教会中学的创立也使这一时期教会学校得以扩张。另外，教会的女子教育也蓬勃发展。神学院、师范学校以及专门的医学校也在这一阶段创办。

◎ 旧时女子学堂的妇女。（陈亚元 供图）
　Women at girls' school in the old days. (Courtesy of Chen Yayuan)

◎ 19世纪末鼓浪屿寄读的女学生。（白桦 供图）

Girl boarders on Kulangsu at the end of the 19th century. (Courtesy of Bai Hua)

Missionary Girls' Schools and Primary Schools

From the 1850s until the establishment of the international settlement, missionaries set up various schools on Kulangsu such as kindergartens, primary schools, high schools, teachers' schools, specialized medical schools, vocational schools, seminaries, and schools for women and refugee children...There were day schools, boarding schools as well as schools for boys and girls. These missionary schools, together with private and public schools run by Chinese, made the small island of Kulangsu home to the highest density of schools in South Fujian. School education on Kulangsu had exerted such an influence that in 1917, the American Reformed Church brought in Wei Shengping, a specialist in children, to set up the department of education of the Church on Kulangsu to lead the missionary schools established by the Church in South Fujian.

Early missionary schools were small, with only a dozen or so students. These schools were usually attached to churches or missionary houses, offering literacy and religious courses in which South Fujian POJ was promoted.

After the second Opium War, the church developed rapidly, and Western education grew with it. Meanwhile, China's Westernization Movement advocated the establishment of modern schools, which brought about changes to the former imperial examination system. More and more students attended missionary schools. At the same time, primary education on Kulangsu began to develop widely, and some schools became co-ed schools, admitting both boys and girls. The establishment of missionary high schools also helped the expansion of missionary schools during this period. In addition, women's missionary education also flourished. Seminaries, teachers' schools and specialized medical schools were also set up.

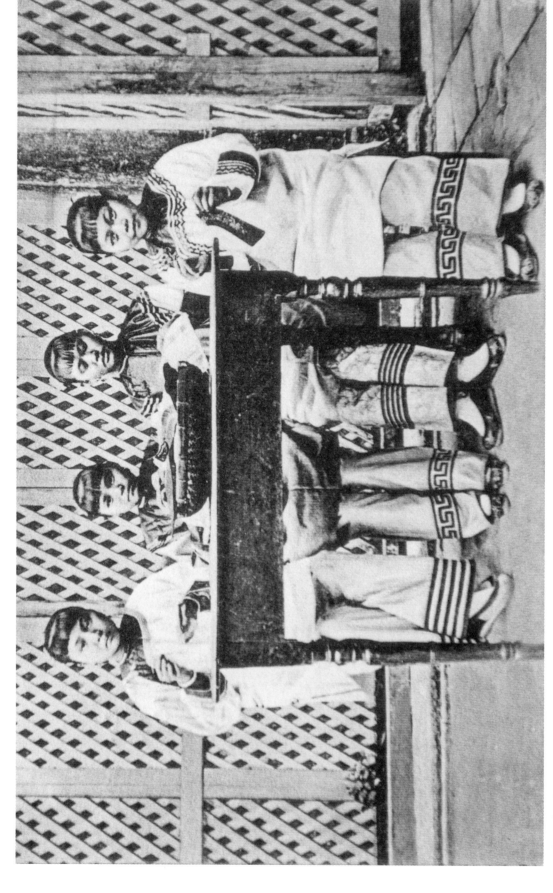

◎ 女子学堂的妇女。（陈亚元 供图）

Women at girls' school. (Courtesy of Chen Yayuan)

1844年，英国伦敦差会传教士施约翰夫妇来到厦门鼓浪屿，在和记崎一带建起三座二层楼房，创办了"福音小学"。三座楼其中一幢的楼下作为鼓浪屿最早的礼拜堂，除了主日礼拜外，其余六天作为小学课室，楼上为牧师住宅。"福音小学"是鼓浪屿最早的西式学校，学校的教师为中国人，有学生二三十人。"福音小学"后与乌埭角的"民立小学"合并为"福民小学"，为鼓浪屿名校。中华人民共和国成立后，"福民小学"改名为"笔山小学"，现并入"人民小学"。

1876年，英国长老会倪为林牧师娘和吴罗宾牧师娘向外募捐，隔年6月在鼓浪屿乌埭角发起创办女学，取名"乌埭女学"，又名"红毛女学"，鼓浪屿人称之为"红毛女学所"。乌埭女学提倡女子教育，招收来自厦漳各地的女寄宿生24名，是福建省最早的寄宿制女校，开创了闽南女子教育的先河。1883年，英国长老会妇女传教协会派安玉瑜姑娘来接办学校。1885年，乌埭女学由仁历西任主理，学生人数已增加到80多人，办学规模逐年扩大。1900年，仁历西开始筹备修建新校舍。1906年，仁历西去世，所以1910年新校舍落成后为了纪念她，学校更名为"怀仁女校"，并于1911年搬迁至永春路（校址即现永春路87号人民小学）。

怀仁女校后增设有初中普通科、高中程度的家事职业学校，曾被日军占领而停办，复办后一度易名鼓浪屿二小。（1951年，怀仁女校与毓德女中合并成厦门鼓浪屿女子中学。）

◎ 1935年鼓浪屿福民小学教职工。（白桦 供图）
The staff of Fumin Primary School, Kulangsu, 1935. (Courtesy of Bai Hua)

◎ 鼓浪屿人民小学。（子健传媒 供图）
People's Primary School, Kulangsu. (Courtesy of Zijian Media)

In 1844, John Stronach and his wife from London Missionary Society came to Kulangsu and built a mansion of three two-story buildings in the neighbourhood of Hejiqi, in which they founded "Evangelical Primary School".

The first floor of one of the three buildings served as the earliest chapels on Kulangsu, which held services on Sundays and was used as a classroom on weekdays and Saturdays. The missionary family lived on the second floor. "Evangelical Primary School" was the earliest modern school on Kulangsu, with Chinese teachers and dozens of students. Later on, it merged with "Minli Primary School" in Wudaijiao to become "Fumin Primary School", a top-tier primary school on Kulangsu. After the founding of the People's Republic of China, the school was renamed "Bishan Primary School" and merged now with "People's Primary School".

◎ 1924年毓德女中丙级毕业生纪念照。（白桦 供图）
Graduate photo of Loktek Girls' School, 1924. (Courtesy of Bai Hua)

In 1876, Mrs. McGregor and others from Presbyterian Church of England managed to raise funds and built Wudai Girls' School on Kulangsu in June the following year. Also known as "Western School for Women" by locals, Wudai Girls' School advocated women's education, enrolling 24 female boarders from all over Amoy and Zhangzhou. It was the first boarding school for women in Fujian Province, marking the beginning of female education in South Fujian. In 1883, Women's Missionary Association of Presbyterian Church of England sent Miss G. Maclagan (An Yuyu) to take over the school. In 1885, Wudai Girls' School was placed under the care of Jessie M. Johnston (Ren Lixi) and the number of students increased to more than 80. In 1900, Jessie M. Johnston began to plan for the construction of a new school building. She died in 1906 and therefore in 1910 when the new school building was completed, the school was renamed "Hoaijin (Huairen) Girls' School" in her memory. In 1911, the school was relocated to Yongchun Road (now People's Primary School, at 87 Yongchun Road).

Hoaijin Girls' School later expanded with the addition of junior high school section and housekeeping vocational school of senior high level, which was suspended due to the occupation by the Japanese army. The school changed its name into "Kulangsu No. 2 Primary School" after it reopened. (In 1951, Hoaijin Girls' School and Loktek Girls' School were merged into Kulangsu Girls' School in Xiamen.)

1879年，创办于1870年的女子日校及寄宿学校毓德学校搬迁到鼓浪屿。美国归正教会打马字牧师的二女儿马利亚·打马字接手学校事务，担任校长。这是厦门第一个小学程度的女学，初始仅有学生12人。

1880年，美国归正教会购置田尾路土地为校址，先后建有大小校舍4座，女学堂迁至鼓浪屿田尾，当时叫"田尾女学堂"，也被称为"花旗女学"。田尾女学堂由小学发展到中学，1889年，改名为"毓德女子小学"。毓德学校的学生不断增多，至1899年便有学生76人，学生的年龄从8岁至21岁皆有。在1870年到1920年的50年里，共有1,500名女学生毕业于毓德学校。

◎ 毓德女学校旧址。（杨戈 摄）
Former Loktek Girls' School. (Photo by Yang Ge)

◎ 养元小学毕业纪念照。（白桦 供图）
Graduate photo of Yangyuan Primary School. (Courtesy of Bai Hua)

　　归正教会还办起了妇学堂——田尾妇女福音学院。这所又叫"田尾妇学堂"的学校创办于1884年，最初名叫"圣经识字班"，创办人及院长是打马字牧师的大女儿清洁·打马字。这个学院是专为已婚妇女而设的，因此学生年龄差距很大。学员的年龄从15岁到70岁都有。1884年开学时学生仅有5人，1889年增至24人，1894年达200人。其中相当一部分还是从漳州、同安和厦门郊区来的，都在学校住宿。

　　1889年，美国归正教会在厦门竹树脚创办了养元小学，后迁到鼓浪屿田尾路，被称为"田尾小学"。学校的创办人兼首任主理是清洁·打马字。养元小学后来再迁鼓浪屿的洋人球埔（今马约翰体育场）边。学校只收男生，不收女生，学生人数曾是全岛小学之冠，有过许多赫赫有名的毕业生：文学家林语堂，天文学家余青松，1926年间任厦门自来水公司总工程师、美国麻省理工学院毕业生林全诚等。

　　1898年，伦敦差会又创办了"民立小学"。1909年，民立小学与福音小学合并，改名为"福民小学"。1912年，福民小学发展为完全小学。

　　1905年，美国安息日会创办了"育粹小学"，后改名为"美华小学"。1910年后，迁往五个牌（现鼓声路12号）的自建校舍，还曾一度扩办了中学。

　　1920年，天主教厦门教区的主教、西班牙多明我会传教士马守仁创办了维正小学，校址设在鼓浪屿博爱路34号。学校后由庞迪仁牧师主理，并增办师范班。

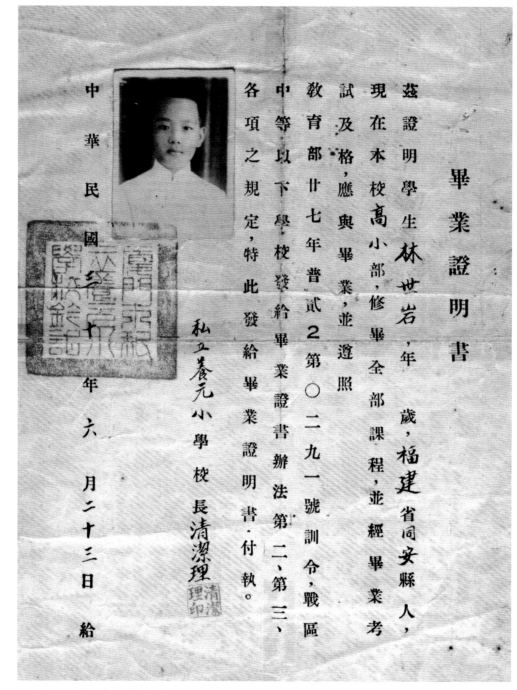

畢業證明書

茲證明學生林世岩，年　歲，福建省同安縣人，現在本校高小部，修畢全部課程，並經畢業考試及格，應與畢業，並遵照教育部廿七年普貳2第○二九一號訓令，戰區中等以下學校發給畢業證書辦法第二、第三、各項之規定，特此發給畢業證明書，付執。

私立養元小學校長清潔理印

中華民國　年六月二十三日給

◎ 养元小学毕业证书。（白桦 供图）
Diploma of Yangyuan Primary School. (Courtesy of Bai Hua)

In 1879, Loktek School, a day and boarding school for girls founded in 1870, was relocated to Kulangsu. M. E. Talmage, the second daughter of American Reformed Church Missionary, Rev. John Van Nest Talmage, took over as its headmaster. It was the first primary school for girls in Amoy, starting with only 12 students.

In 1880, the American Reformed Church purchased a piece of land on Tianwei Road as the school site, and built 4 school houses over time. The girls' school was then moved to the new site with the name "Tianwei Girls' School" or "Huaqi Girls' School". Developed from a primary school to one with an attached high school, the school was renamed "Loktek (Yude) Girls' Primary School" in 1889 drawing an increasing number of students. In 1899 there were 76 students, ranging in age from 8 to 21. In the 50 years from 1870 to 1920, a total of 1,500 female students graduated from Loktek Girls' School.

The Reformed Church also founded the Tianwei Gospel School for Women in 1884 which was named "Scripture Reading Class" initially. Established and run by K. M. Talmage, the first daughter of Rev. John Van Nest Talmage, the school was for married women, and had students of ages ranging from 15 to 70. There were only five students when the school was first opened in 1884. The number increased to 24 in 1889 and 200 in 1894. Quite a few of them came from Zhangzhou, Tong'an and the suburbs of Amoy and therefore boarded at school.

In 1889, the American Reformed Church established Yangyuan Primary School at Zhushujiao in Amoy, which was relocated to Tianwei Road on Kulangsu, known as "Tianwei Primary School", with K. M. Talmage as the founder and first headmaster. The school was later relocated again to the site by Foreigners' Football Field (now Ma Yuehan Stadium). The school only enrolled male students, and the enrollment once topped all primary schools on the island. The school turned out many excellent graduates, such as Lin Yutang the writer, Yu Qingsong the astronomer and Lin Quancheng, chief engineer of Amoy Water Supply Company in 1926 and graduate of Massachusetts Institute of Technology.

In 1898, the London Missionary Society founded Minli Primary School, which merged with Gospel Primary School in 1909 and was renamed "Fumin Primary School". In 1912, the school developed into a complete primary school.

In 1905, American Sabbath Church founded Yucui Primary School, which was later renamed Meihua (American-Chinese) Primary School. After 1910, the school was relocated to houses built by the church on the piece of land "Wugepai" (now at 12 Gusheng Road) and expanded with an attached high school.

In 1920, Manuel Prat, Bishop of the Catholic Amoy Diocese and missionary of Spanish Catholic Ordo Dominicanorum, founded Weizheng Primary School at 34 Pok Oi Road, Kulangsu. The school was later run by Rev. Pang Diren and expanded to train teachers.

教会所办的中学

为了让教会小学毕业的学生可以继续上学，让小学有教师来源，也让教会的神学院有合格的学生来源，1881年1月，大英长老会和美国归正教会在鼓浪屿田尾创办了"男童学院"——鼓浪屿最早的中学，俗称"寻源斋"。学校最初是在一座重修的属于大英长老会的华人房子里办学，课程介于小学和女子学校之间，以"中学"为名，并有一个"寻源"的中文名称，意即"寻找真理的源泉"。

寻源校风十分严谨，注重教学质量和重视学生成绩。新生入学都要进行考试筛选，不达标准的淘汰。学校收学杂费都比公立学校高。学校初办期间（1889），一个学生每学期交学杂费24元银圆。抗日战争期间（1943），每生学杂费120元（约一钱黄金价值）。到校上学的大部分是工商业者、医生、教师等较富裕家庭的子女。但对基督教会牧师等人的子女，如家庭经济有困难，学杂费则可酌情减免。

为了方便远地农村的学生，寻源中学后改为寄宿学校，要求所有学生都须寄宿。学校学制三年，课程包括《新约》《旧约》《史记》和《诗经》、闽南白话字的认识和书写、书法、历史（中国和英国）、地理学、生理学、天文学基本原理、算术、代数学和自然地理学。在毕腓力夫人的教导下，学生们还学会了不用仪器绘制地图。后来学校还增加了一些新的科目，包括英语、高等数学、生物学、医学，并增加了古典名著的科目。

◎ 20世纪20年代的寻源中学校舍。（白桦 供图）
Xunyuan Academy in the 1920s. (Courtesy of Bai Hua)

Missionary High Schools

To provide opportunities for graduates from the missionary primary schools to continue with their school education, as well as to staff primary schools with teachers and to build a source of qualified students to be enrolled by the seminary of the church, the British Presbyterian Church and the American Reformed Church established a boys' institute in Tianwei in January 1881. This was the earliest high school on Kulangsu, commonly known as Xunyuan Academy. The school was first opened in a restored Chinese house belonging to the British Presbyterian Church and offered courses this way or that of a primary school and a girls'

◎ 英华书院教师楼。（子健传媒 供图）
Teacher building of Anglo-Chinese College (Yinghua Academy). (Courtesy of Zijian Media)

school. It was named "high school" and the Chinese "Xunyuan" (seeking the source) had the implication of "seeking the source of truth".

With a carefully managed school culture and a strong emphasis on quality teaching and student achievement, Xunyuan Academy carried out the practice of entrance examination screening for new enrolments, so that those not up to the standard would not be admitted, and it charged more for tuition and fees than public schools did. During the early days of the school (1889), a student had to pay 24 silver dollars per semester for tuition and miscellaneous fees. During the War of Resistance against Japanese Aggression (1943), the charge was 120 yuan (about the value of five grams of gold) per student. Most students who could afford were children of wealthy families such as businessmen, doctors and teachers. However, tuition and miscellaneous fees could be waived for children from needy pastor and priest families.

Taking into consideration that some students came from remote rural areas, Xunyuan High School was later changed into a boarding school, requiring boarding for all students. The school was a three-year program offering courses such as *The New Testament*, *The Old Testament*, *Shih Chi* and the *Book of Songs*, literacy of POJ of South Fujian Dialect (the earliest Romanization of Chinese characters), calligraphy, history (Chinese and English), geography, physiology, fundamentals of astronomy, arithmetic, algebra and physical geography. Under the guidance of Mrs. Philip Wilson Pitcher, the students also learned to map without instruments. Later, new subjects were added to the curriculum, including English, advanced mathematics, biology, medicine, and classics.

1890年后，寻源效仿美国的中学将学制增加一年。寻源不仅汇聚了许多优秀的教师，学校的教学设施也颇为完备。学校设有田径、球类设施，还有音乐室、图书室、实验室、标本室。音乐室有钢琴、风琴和各式铜管乐器，图书室有报刊、图书等，学生可阅读多种名著及教学参考资料；实验室里有力学、电学等实验仪器和化学药剂；标本室有飞禽、爬虫类等动物标本。寻源学生的英语水平高，据说曾有一位美籍教师卜英典不会讲汉语，上课都讲英语，学生亦能勉强听懂。当时学生刘植树翻译了一篇外国文学作品，刊登在厦门《江声报》；学生卓世华能与学校的美国董事流利对话。1920年，寻源中学还办了为学生实习而设的教孺园。

　　因此，要求来寻源入学的学生逐渐增多，1922年已有在校学生245人。寻源中学办学成绩良好，如每年只收25名学生的北京协和医学院1921年就招了两名寻源的毕业生进入，另有三分之一的寻源毕业生被列入候补名单。而升入厦门大学、福建协和大学、广州岭南大学以及本地神学院的学生也不少。在寻源中学毕业的莘莘学子中，出了不少专家、教授、学者。如29岁获得博士学位、提出太阳系起源新学说的世界著名天文学家戴文赛，把大量东方文化介绍给西方的著名翻译家、文学家林语堂，我国神经外科奠基人赵以成，农业遗传学专家林建兴等，都是在寻源中学就读时打下基础的。据说，因为当年从漳州来寻源读书的学生不少——林语堂就是其中一个，所以寻源书院所在的这一条路就得名"漳州路"。

◎　1915年寻源书院全体师生合影。（白桦　供图）

All the teachers and students of Xunyuan Academy, 1915. (Courtesy of Bai Hua)

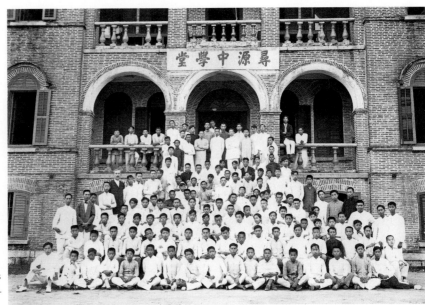

◎ 1916年寻源书院全体师
　生合影。（白桦 供图）
All the teachers and students
of Xunyuan Academy, 1916.
(Courtesy of Bai Hua)

After 1890, Xunyuan added one year of schooling following the practice in the United States. The school had gathered many excellent teachers with full teaching facilities, such as track and field grounds, playing grounds for ball games, a music room, library, laboratory and specimen room. There were pianos, organs and various brass instruments in the music room; newspapers and books in the library so that students could read a variety of classics and reference materials. The laboratory provided experimental instruments for dynamics, electricity and chemical agents while in the specimen room there were birds, reptiles and other animal specimens. It was said that students in Xunyuan spoke very good English and there was an American teacher who could not speak Chinese and conducted the class in English. One of the students Liu Zhishu even translated a piece of foreign literature and got it published in *Jiangsheng* (Wave Sound) *Daily* in Amoy. Another student Zhuo Shihua could speak fluently in English with the school's American board directors. In 1920, Xunyuan also opened a kindergarten as a base for the students' internship.

As a result, the number of students seeking for admission to the school increased, and the enrolment was 245 in 1922. The school had stellar record. For example, Peking Union Medical College, which had an annual enrolment of only 25 students, admitted two graduates from Xunyuan in 1921, and a third of them were placed on the waiting list. There were also quite a few graduates going to Amoy University, Fujian Union University, Lingnan University in Guangzhou and local seminaries for further studies. Many graduates from Xunyuan later became experts, professors and scholars. Among others, there were Dai Wensai, a world-renowned astronomer who received a doctoral degree at the age of 29 and put forward a new theory on the origin of the solar system; Lin Yutang, a famous writer and translator who introduced a great deal of Oriental culture to the Western world; Zhao Yicheng, the founder of China's neurosurgery; and Lin Jianxing, an agricultural geneticist. They all received solid educational foundations in Xunyuan. It was said that many students came from Zhangzhou—and Lin Yutang was one of them—so the road where the academy was located was named "Zhangzhou Road".

◎ 20世纪20年代的英华书院。（白桦 供图）

Anglo-Chinese College, Amoy, in the 1920s. (Courtesy of Bai Hua)

　　1898年2月28日，英国伦敦圣公会的山雅各牧师在鼓浪屿笔架山麓荔枝宅（现安海路6号）附近创办英华书院。学校最初设置为英国学制的高等学堂，并附设大学预科二年。中科院和工程院原院士王应睐、现任院士卓仁禧，科学家谢希仁、朱晓屏、陈慰中，历史学家韩振华、陈国强，经济学家吴宣恭，体育教育家陈安怀，华侨将军黄登保，爱国华侨实业家黄琢齐、黄望青、陈并茂等，都是二十世纪三四十年代英华书院培养出来的知名校友。

　　1910年，美国安息日会创办的美华小学（原育粹小学）在自建校舍后，扩办为中学。1934年，在鸡山路5号增办美华女校。1938年，男女两校合并，迁入新建的安献堂内，改名为"美华三育研究社"，学校设英、汉、算三科。20世纪20年代到日本人占领鼓浪屿之前，是美华中学的黄金时代。学校有实验室、图书馆，学生穿着统一的校服、佩戴校徽，学校还制定了校歌和校训。美华还办了美华农场和牛奶场。奶牛是引进荷兰的良种奶牛，根据美国牛奶场的生产方式管理。奶牛食用的草料也从国外引进，在山地上种植。牛奶不仅质量有保证，包装也讲究。包装瓶和封口蜡纸也从美国进口。牛奶瓶标上"美华牛奶场"标签后，每天按时专人送到订户家里。美华农场的蔬菜优质新鲜，菜贩争着来买。学校还在山上挖了两口深井，架设了两台美式风车，车叶随风不停地转，上下抽水，这算是岛上最早的"自来水"。

On February 28, 1898, Rev. James Sadler of the London Missionary Society set up Anglo-Chinese College (Yinghua Academy) near Litchi Residence in Bijia Hill, Kulangsu (now at 6 Anhai Road). The school was originally set up as an English institution of higher learning with two years of preparatory courses. Former and current academicians of the Chinese Academy of Sciences and Chinese Academy of Engineering Wang Yinglai and Zhuo Renxi; scientists Xie Xiren, Zhu Xiaoping and Chen Weizhong; historians Han Zhenhua and Chen Guoqiang; economist Wu Xuangong; sports educator Chen Anhuai; overseas Chinese general Huang Dengbao; patriotic overseas Chinese entrepreneurs Huang Zhuoqi, Huang Wangqing and Chen Bingmao were all outstanding alumni from the 1930s and 1940s.

In 1910, Meihua (American-Chinese) Primary School (formerly "Yucui Primary School") built by the American Sabbath Church was expanded to a high school on its own premises. In 1934, Meihua Girls' School was established at 5 Jishan Road. The two schools merged in 1938 and moved into the newly built Anxian Hall to become "Meihua Education Research Society", offering English, Chinese and mathematics. The 1920s was a golden age for Meihua High School before the Japanese occupation. The school provided a laboratory and a library. Students wore school uniform and badges and there were school anthem and motto. Meihua also ran its own vegetable farm and dairy farm. Cows were of fine breeds introduced from the Netherlands and were raised according to the practices of dairy farms in the United States. Forage for the cattle was also introduced from abroad and planted in the hills. The milk was not only guaranteed in quality, but also finely packaged. Packaging bottles and sealing wax paper were also imported from the US. Labeled "Meihua Dairy", milk bottles were delivered to customers' homes on time every day. Meihua Farm was known for its high quality fresh vegetables that were sought by vegetable vendors. The school also dug two deep wells in the hill going with two American-style watermills, whose blades kept turning with the wind to pump water up and down. This was the earliest "tap water" on the island.

◎ 美华中学旧址。（子健传媒 供图）
Former Meihua (American-Chinese) High School. (Courtesy of Zijian Media)

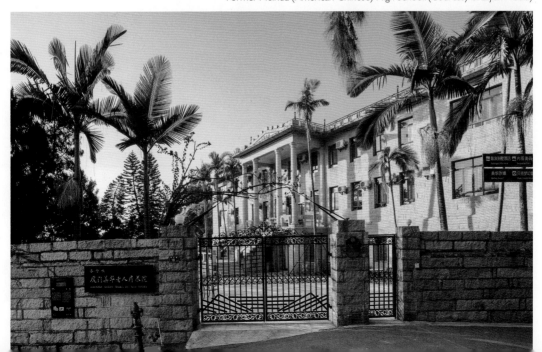

中国第一所幼儿园和为传教服务的神学院

日光岩下的怀德幼稚园——如今的日光幼儿园，是基督教在中国创办的第一所儿童教育机构，也是中国历史上第一所现代意义的幼儿园。

1898年，在鼓浪屿传教的大英长老会韦玉振牧师的夫人韦爱莉创办了家庭幼稚园，最初的园址在鼓浪屿维新路35号牧师楼，后来迁至鼓浪屿内厝澳西路（现永春路83号）新建的园舍。

1910年，大英长老会接办幼稚园。1911年，将其命名为"怀德幼稚园"。

怀德幼稚园主要招收4岁到6岁的基督教徒子女入园受教育，按年龄分班。历任园

◎ 日光幼儿园。（子健传媒 供图）
Sunlight Kindergarten. (Courtesy of Zijian Media)

长都是大英长老会派来的女教士，老师则基本是岛上教会学校的毕业生，同时也是基督徒。

怀德幼稚园教育条件很好，教学所使用的教具、教材全部由英国运来，实行的是教育家蒙台梭利的教育模式，主张用玩具开发儿童的智力，利用20种她发明的玩具（称为"恩物"）发展儿童的感觉器官，学习数学、自然科学、语言文学、绘画、手工、唱歌及宗教知识等。怀德幼稚园创办之后，厦门的各外国教会相继仿效，在厦门的竹树脚、泰山口、新街等陆续办起幼稚园。

◎ 1935年怀德幼稚园毕业生留影纪念。（白桦 供图）
Graduate photo of Huaide Kindergarten, 1935. (Courtesy of Bai Hua)

◎ 幼儿在上课。（白桦 供图）

Children in class. (Courtesy of Bai Hua)

China's First Kindergarten and Mission-Serving Seminary

At the foot of Sunlight Rock lies Huaide Kindergarten, now known as Sunlight Kindergarten, which was the first children's educational institution founded by Christianity in China and the first modern kindergarten in Chinese history.

In 1898, Alice Wales, wife of Rev. George M. Wales of the British Presbyterian Church preaching on Kulangsu, founded a family kindergarten, which was originally located in the vicarage building at 35 Weixin Road, Kulangsu, and later moved to the newly built house on West Neicuo'ao Road (now at 83 Yongchun Road) .

In 1910, the British Presbyterian Church took over the kindergarten and named it Huaide Kindergarten in 1911.

The kindergarten mainly enrolled Christian children aged 4 to 6 and ran accordingly divided classes. All the headmasters were priestesses sent by the British Presbyterian Church and most teachers were graduates of missionary schools on the island.

Huaide Kindergarten enjoyed excellent teaching facilities, with materials and textbooks carried from Britain by ship, and following the practice of education advocated by Maria Montessori, an Italian woman doctor and educator, who claimed that toys were the best things to develop children's intelligence. 20 kinds of toys she invented (known as "boons") were used to develop the sense organs of children and help them learn mathematics, natural science, language, literature, painting, handwork, singing and religion, among others. After the establishment of Huaide Kindergarten, foreign churches in Amoy followed suit and set up kindergartens in Zhushujiao, Taishankou and Xinjie.

◎ 1928年闽南圣道专门大学第二届毕业纪念。（白桦 供图）

Graduate photo of 2nd Class, Holy Bible University, 1928. (Courtesy of Bai Hua)

为了培养幼儿园的师资，1901年，大英长老会在怀德幼稚园内附设了幼稚师范班。1912年，创办幼稚师范学校，称为"怀德幼师"，为闽南各地的启蒙幼稚学堂培养师资，校址在鼓浪屿漳州路，学校的学生大部分来自怀仁女中毕业生。厦门解放后怀德幼师停办。

起初，中国的传教士和牧师都是在一些外国传教士家里接受培训，为培养中国籍牧师，19世纪50年代，教会办起了专门的圣道学校。

伦敦差会创办的是观澜斋，校舍在内厝澳。1869年，归正教会在鼓浪屿建起了一座两层红砖楼，有一间讲堂、十一间卧室和一间厨房的回澜圣道学院，校址在龙坑井安海路（今安海路）。1907年，两所神学校合并为回澜圣道学院，这是福建最早的神学院。第二年，改称"圣道大学"，规定只有中学毕业生才能就读。校舍先在厦门邦坪尾，后迁至鼓浪屿内厝澳，又迁往岩仔脚。1919年停办。

1917年，中华基督教大会闽南大会将英国长老会办的泉州福音学校和寻源中学的道学科合并，由闽南大会和英美三公会在鼓浪屿合办神学院，并分为甲乙两级。1937年，神学院迁往漳州马公庙。1939年，改名为"闽南神学院"。1951年，并入南京金陵神学院。

1922年以后，中国人自办的新式学校如武荣中学等和教会学校并存，是鼓浪屿的一大特点。这也使得鼓浪屿的中、小学校数量之多，其密度之高居于全国前列，并且在闽南、台湾以及东南亚等地颇有影响。

In order to prepare kindergarten teachers, the British Presbyterian Church set up an attached class for the training of such teachers in 1901. In 1912, the class was expanded to become "Huaide Kindergarten Teachers School" to prepare teaching staff for preschool education in South Fujian. The school was located on Zhangzhou Road, Kulangsu. Most of the students in the school were graduates from Hoaijin Girls' School. Huaide Kindergarten Teachers School was suspended after the liberation of Amoy in 1949.

At first, Chinese missionaries and priests were trained in the homes of some foreign missionaries. In the 1850s, churches began to set up special missionary schools for the training of Chinese pastors.

The London Missionary Society founded Guanlan Bible School in Neicuo'ao. In 1869, the Reformed Church built a two-storey red-brick building called Huilan Holy Bible Academy on Anhai Road, Longkengjing, Kulangsu, with a lecture hall, 11 bedrooms and a kitchen. In 1907, the two divinity schools merged into one bearing the same name as Huilan Bible Academy which was the earliest seminary in Fujian. The school was renamed Holy Bible University the following year and admitted only secondary school graduates. The schoolhouse was first located in Bangpingwei, Amoy, and was relocated to Neicuo'ao, and then to Yanzijiao. It was suspended in 1919.

In 1917, the China Christian Congress South Fujian Committee merged Quanzhou Gospel School run by the British Presbyterian Church and the Theology Department of Xunyuan High School to jointly establish a seminary on Kulangsu together with Three Societies co-founded by the American Reformed Church, London Missionary Society and British Presbyterian Church. The school was divided into two grades of A and B. In 1937, the seminary moved to Magong Temple in Zhangzhou and was renamed South Fujian Seminary in 1939. In 1951, the school was incorporated into Nanjing Jinling Seminary.

Since 1922, modern schools run by the Chinese such as Wurong High School had coexisted with foreign missionary schools, which was one of the features of Kulangsu. As a result, there was a high density of secondary and primary schools despite the size of Kulangsu. This also added to the influence of Kulangsu in South Fujian, Taiwan and Southeast Asia.

闽南白话字与印刷出版业

在医疗救治、办学和传教的过程中，西方传教士们慢慢去接近和理解另一种原本对他们来说完全陌生的语言——闽南语，并由此产生了闽南白话字。闽南白话字是厦门话的拉丁字母拼音方案，共有23个字母，17个声母，65个韵母（其中普通韵母31个，鼻化韵11个，入声韵23个）。闽南白话字易学易写，只要能念出读音就可以写出文字，"短则一个星期，长则一个月，就能掌握，再经过三五个月到半年，就能熟练地阅读《圣经》了。"

1832年，西方人研究闽南方言的开拓先锋，也是用罗马字拼音表记录闽南方言的开创者麦都思在马六甲完成第一本闽南语罗马字字典《汉语福建方言字典》。此后，在厦门传教45年的打马字牧师出版了《唐话翻字初学》和《厦门音字典》；罗啻编写了《英汉厦门方言罗马注音手册》，这是第一部标明汉英厦门方言的字典，在新加坡、台湾流传很广；杜嘉德的《厦英大辞典》、麦嘉湖的《英华口才集》《英厦辞典》、偕叙理的《中西字典》、甘为霖的《厦门音新字典》、巴克礼的《厦英大辞典增补》都是关于白话字的著作。

白话字不但风行闽南各地，也传到吕宋岛、新加坡、槟榔屿等，为当地华侨所用。白话字还走出鼓浪屿，去到西方——1873年，罗啻牧师译成白话字的《旧约全书》《新约全书》在英国刊印。用白话字翻译的《字汇入门》《四书解释》《三字经译诠》等汉学书籍亦相继问世。

◎ 打马字牧师。（白桦 供图）

Rev. John V. N. Talmage, D. D.（Courtesy of Bai Hua）

South Fujian POJ and Printing Industry

Through their experience in preaching, medical treatment and management of schools, Western missionaries began to learn the South Fujian dialect (Hokkien), a language which was completely unbeknownst to them, and they invented South Fujian POJ, the Romanization of Chinese characters in Amoy vernacular with the Latin alphabet system. Consisting of 23 letters, 17 initial consonants and 65 simple or compound vowels (including 31 ordinary vowels, 11 nasal rhymes and 23 rhymes), South Fujian POJ was easy to learn and write. As long as one could read out the pronunciation, he could write out the words. "It takes a week or a month to grasp. And after another three or six months to practice, one could read the *Bible* fluently."

In 1832, Walter Henry Medhurst, one of the Western pioneers of South Fujian dialect studies and inventors of writing Chinese in South Fujian dialect by the use of the Latin alphabets, finished in Malacca his writing of *A Dictionary of the Hok-keen Dialect of the Chinese Language, According to the Reading and Colloquial Idioms*, the first dictionary of the romanized South Fujian vernacular. This was followed by many other publications on POJ, including *Introduction to Amoy Alphabets* and *The Amoy Colloquial Dictionary* by Rev. John Van Nest Talmage, who served as a missionary in Amoy for 45 years; *Anglo-Chinese Manual with Romanized Colloquial in the Amoy Dialect* by Rev. Elihu Doty, the first dictionary to employ a romanized system to write South Fujian dialect which was popular in Singapore and Taiwan; *Chinese-English Dictionary of the Vernacular or Spoken Language of Amoy* by Cartairs Douglas; *A Manual of the Amoy Colloquial* and *English and Chinese Dictionary of the Amoy Dialect* by John Macgowan; *Chinese Romanized Dictionary of the Formosan Vernacular* by George Leslie Mackay; *A Dictionary of the Amoy Vernacular* by W. Campbell and *A Supplement to Chinese-English Dictionary of the Vernacular or Spoken Language of Amoy* by Thomas Barclay.

◎ 英国长老会牧师杜嘉德。（白桦 供图）
Rev. Cartairs Douglas with British Presbyterian Church. （Courtesy of Bai Hua）

POJ, or the romanized Amoy vernacular, not only gained popularity in South Fujian, but also spread to Luzon Island, Singapore and Penang Island to be used by overseas Chinese. It even went west. In 1873, *The Old Testament* and *The New Testament*, translated into POJ by Rev. Elihu Doty, were printed and published in England. Other Chinese classics, such as *Introduction to Chinese Characters, Interpretations of the Four Books,* and *Interpretations of the Three Character Primer,* were also translated into POJ and published.

◎ 1900年轮船公司英文期刊刊登《厦门教会学堂的女同学，正在放学的路上》。（白桦 供图）
A work named *Girl Students on the Way Back Home* on the English magazine published by the Steamship Company, 1900.（Courtesy of Bai Hua）

　　1908年，中外基督教徒们共同组织了"圣教书局董事会"，并在鼓浪屿的大埭路（现龙头路446号）开办了闽南圣教书局——中国当时六家圣教书局之一，也是闽南地区唯一的非纯营利性质的宗教书局。1932年，教会人士捐献地皮和经费，在福建路（现福建路43号）建了一幢三层楼房，作为书局新址。

　　来厦门传教的教会还办起了不少报纸刊物，加上驻厦领事馆、外国人办的其他报纸，使厦门的报业在清朝末年兴起。早在1878年，鼓浪屿就已经出版了两份外文报刊，一份是《厦门公报与航运报》，每日出版；另一份汉语译为《闲话双月刊》，这两份报刊的内容全是外文。1886年，英国传教士布德创办了《厦门新报》，这是厦门的第一份中文月刊。《厦门新报》主要刊载时事新闻和教会新闻，用厦门方言写作。1888年，打马字牧师夫妇在鼓浪屿创办了《漳泉公会报》，后改名《闽南圣会报》，每月出版，也用厦门方言写作，刊载的主要内容为教会消息，历任经理和主笔均由外国神职人员担任，1938年改为闽南白话、汉文对照。这些报刊中影响较大的要数英国牧师山雅各创办的《鹭江报》。《鹭江报》是当时英国驻厦门领事馆通过基督教会办的报刊，于光绪二十八年三月二十一日创刊，光绪二十八年八月二十八日发行。牧师山雅各任总经理兼总主笔，其余13名编辑人员基本上是厦鼓的知名人士或者基督教徒，如麦嘉湖、卢戆章等，连横也曾担任此报的主笔。

　　此外，还有天主教创办的《公教周刊》、闽南美国公理会的《教育通讯》《教育世界》《指南针》《石生》，厦门基督教青年会印行的《厦门青年》，还有厦门毓德女子中学出版的《毓德校刊》、厦门鼓浪屿福民学校的《福闽声》和《道南报》等。

　　教会频繁出版报刊，大量印行书籍，在某种程度上促进了鼓浪屿以及厦门印刷业的发展。鼓浪屿其时有经营印刷业务的萃经堂和启新印书局，因此像翟理斯这样的外国人居住在鼓浪屿，才能够准时在黄昏的餐桌上读到当地印刷出版的报纸，得享丰富的精神食粮。

In 1908, Chinese and foreign Christians jointly organized the "Board of Religious Tract Society", and set up the Bookstore of South Fukien Religious Tract Society on Dadai Road (now at 446 Longtou Road) on Kulangsu—one of the six bookstores of religious tract societies in China at the time and the only non-profit religious bookstore in South Fujian. In 1932, church members donated land and funds to build a three-storey building at 43 Fujian Road as a new site for the bookstore.

Missionaries coming to Amoy also ran a number of newspapers, which, together with other newspapers run by consulates and foreigners in Amoy, gave rise to the local press industry in the late Qing Dynasty. As early as in 1878, Kulangsu had two newspapers: one was the daily *Amoy Gazette and Shipping News* and the other was *Gossip Bimonthly,* both written in English. In 1886, British missionary C. Budd founded *Amoy Monthly,* which was the first Chinese monthly magazine in Amoy. Covering news about current affairs and church events, the magazine was written in the Amoy dialect. In 1888, Rev. John Van Nest Talmage and Mrs. Talmage started *Zhangzhou-Quanzhou Gazette* on Kulangsu, which was later renamed *South Fujian Holy Society Gazette.* Written also in the Amoy dialect and covering news about church activities, the monthly was managed and contributed to by foreign missionaries. In 1938, it was changed to a bilingual version, including the South Hokkien vernacular writing and Chinese characters as the other language. The most influential of these newspapers was *Law Kang Po* run by the British missionary Rev. James Sadler. Commissioned by the British consulate in Amoy, the newspaper first came out on March 21, 1902, the 28th year of the reign of Emperor Guangxu, and was distributed on August 28 of the same year. Rev. James Sadler acted as the general manager and editor-in-chief, and the 13 editors were mostly prominent figures or Christians, including John Macgowan and Lu Zhuangzhang. Lien Heng, Lien Chan's grandfather and a well-known writer, was once the chief editor of the newspaper.

In addition, there were the *Catholic Weekly* run by the Catholic Church; *Education Newsletter, World of Education, The Compass* and *Shi Sheng* by American Congregational Church in South Fujian; *Amoy Youth* by Amoy Young Men's Christian Association and *Loktek School Magazine* by Loktek Girls' School as well as *Hokkien Voice* and *Daonan News* by Fumin School on Kulangsu.

The church's frequent publication of newspapers and books boosted the development of the printing industry on Kulangsu and Amoy. There were printing businesses such as "Cuijing House" and Qixin Press on Kulangsu. It was with them that foreign islanders like Herbert Allen Giles were able to do some reading of local newspapers at the dinner table in the evening to satisfy his mind as well as his stomach.

◎ 琴岛小夜曲。（朱庆福 摄）
Night at Piano Island. (Photo by Zhu Qingfu)

音乐体育——永不止息的回响

　　"琴岛"是鼓浪屿的别称，也是许多人对鼓浪屿的美好印象。鼓浪屿人均拥有钢琴的数量堪称中国第一，也因之得名"琴岛"。在百年的悠悠时光里，鼓浪屿的琴音乐声悠扬，穿越过岁月沧桑，依然回响在岛屿的街巷角落里。

　　在日光岩上镌刻下"鹭江第一"的林鍼，既是近代中国赴美的第一人，也是近代最早接触西洋乐器的中国人，他所著的《西海纪游草》一书中介绍了很多西洋新鲜事物，其中就有风琴。他大概未曾预料到，几十年过后，鼓浪屿会成为西洋人聚集的天堂，而那些新鲜的西洋乐器，在岛上已是寻常物。

　　1908年，清政府在厦门接待美国东方舰队来华访问，14岁的鼓浪屿少女周淑安用英文领唱了美国国歌《星条旗永不落》，令美国来访者大吃一惊。

　　从漳州乡村来到鼓浪屿求学的林语堂，也曾被鼓浪屿的音乐所吸引，"我对西洋音乐着实着了迷。我是受了美国校长毕牧师夫人的影响。她是一位端庄淑雅的英国女士，她说话的温柔悦耳抑扬顿挫，我两耳听来，不啻音乐之美。传教士女士们的女高音合唱，在我这个中国人的耳朵听来，真是印象深刻，毕生难忘。"

　　而体育的优良种子，同样随着西人定居鼓浪屿而来，随后经教会和教会学校推广，在鼓浪屿肥沃的土壤里生根发芽，展现永恒旺盛的生命力。

Ongoing Glory: Island of Music and Sports

"**P**iano Island" is another name for Kulangsu as well as the beautiful impression the island leaves on many visitors. Indeed, Kulangsu boasts the highest piano ownership per capita in China, hence the name. Over the course of over one hundred years, music has always been echoing in the streets and corners of the island despite the great changes of the past.

Lin Zhen, who had his inscription "Lu Jiang Di Yi" (Unrivalled Land of Lujiang) carved on Sunlight Rock, was one of the earliest Chinese scholars visiting the US to have access to Western musical instruments in China's modern times. In his book *Records on the Travel in the Western Sea*, he gave accounts of many things exotic to Chinese, including pipe organs. He would not have expected that decades later, Kulangsu would become a paradise where Western people happily gathered, and Western musical instruments turned out to be a common sight on the island.

In 1908, when the Qing Government hosted the visiting US Eastern Fleet to China in Amoy, Zhou Shu'an, a 14-year-old girl from Kulangsu, gave a surprise welcome to the visitors by singing in English *The Star-Spangled Banner*.

Lin Yutang, who came to Kulangsu for school education from the rural area of Zhangzhou, was also attracted by the music of Kulangsu. He later recalled, "I was really fascinated by Western music. This was influenced by my American headmaster Mrs. Anna Pitcher. She was a demure English lady, speaking with a soft, melodious cadence that was musical to my ears. The soprano chorus of the missionary ladies, to my Chinese ears, was very impressive and will never be forgotten."

The seeds of sports also came along with the Westerners who settled down on Kulangsu. It took root and germinated in the fertile soil of the island and was nourished by churches and missionary schools to grow with lasting vitality.

◎ 旧洋人球埔，现为马约翰体育场。（康伦恩 摄）
Former Foreigners' Football Field (now Ma Yuehan Stadium). (Photo by Kang Lun'en)

音乐的启蒙与传播

西洋音乐来到鼓浪屿，首先是以宗教音乐的形式出现的。

德·琼格所著的《归正教会在中国》中有这样的记载："尽管中国人热心参加唱歌，但有些时候宁可参加像乐队那样能获得荣誉的合唱。1900年底到厦门的苑礼文牧师在出席过三、四次华语布道会以后报告说：'这些中国礼拜堂的唱歌非常像我们荷兰教堂的演唱圣诗，每个人都尽其所能地唱得很好，很大声。'"

书中还写到，当年鼓浪屿礼拜天的宗教活动中有一个"最独特的就是所谓的'中国每月音乐会'。这个音乐会于1846年1月5日首次举办，从此以后每个月的第一个星期天举办一次。和伦敦差会以及后来大英长老会的传教士所支持的众多的宗教活动一样，它性质上也是普世的。"

翟理斯在《鼓浪屿简史》中记载，1878年的鼓浪屿已经有管风琴演奏出的悠扬乐声。这一年，鼓浪屿最早的礼拜堂——协和礼拜堂的礼拜开始使用管风琴，由英国人边阿兰司琴。

◎ 1941年三一堂第六届庆祝圣诞歌颂团留影。（白桦 供图）

Singing choir for the sixth Christmas celebration at the Trinity Church. (Courtesy of Bai Hua)

◎ 三一堂音乐会留影。（白桦 供图）
Concert at Trinity Church. (Courtesy of Bai Hua)

Development and Spread of Music

Western music on Kulangsu started in the form of religious music.

According to Gerald Francis De Jong's book, *The Reformed Church in China*, "Although Chinese people are very enthusiastic about singing, joining a choir may give them a sense of achievement and pride. Rev. Abe Livingston Warnsuis, who came to Amoy in late 1900, wrote in a report after he attended a few evangelistic meetings in Chinese: 'The singing in these Chinese churches is very much like our choirs in Dutch churches. Everyone sings as well and loudly as they can.'"

The book also gave an account of "One of Kulangsu's most unique Sunday service events, namely, the 'Chinese Monthly Concert'. The event was first organized on January 5, 1846, and had been held on the first Sunday every month since then. It was welcoming of all, as were many religious activities supported by the London Missionary Society and later by the missionaries of the British Presbyterian Church."

It was recorded in *A Short History of Koolangsu* by Herbert Allen Giles that in 1878, pipe organs began to appear on Kulangsu. In this year, Union Church, the earliest church on the island, began to use the organ to accompany the choir, with A. W. Bain, a Briton, as the organist.

1906年，毓德女学因为唱诗班的需要，从欧洲运来了一架管风琴。这架从欧洲运到鼓浪屿的管风琴，一直放在岩仔脚基督教会福音堂内，供教会唱诗时用，为教徒合唱团伴奏。这架管风琴造型奇特，带有鼓风机，琴体与人齐高，弹琴时需两人配合，一人鼓风，另一人弹奏，才能发出琴音。这架稀奇的乐器成为当时岛上一景。

1913年，台湾富绅、菽庄花园主人林尔嘉从欧洲买了一架真正的钢琴，用作家居装饰陈列。这便是鼓浪屿第一架钢琴。自此以后，岛上的富商纷纷效仿林尔嘉购买钢琴。三一堂和教会创办的学校也先后购置钢琴。鼓浪屿上钢琴的数量逐渐增多，其拥有钢琴的密度以人口平均计算，不仅在国内独占鳌头，在世界上亦罕见。在20世纪二三十年代，西洋音乐已十分盛行的鼓浪屿，名扬海内外，被誉为"音乐岛"。

教堂里的宗教活动，总有唱诗节目，需要有钢琴伴奏。教会学校开设教唱圣诗的课程，亦时常举办文艺活动与比赛。音乐也成了学校一项受欢迎的课外活动，并且时常作为独特的手段为奉献福音启示服务。一场为中国人表演的别具一格的文娱节目献演于1921年的圣诞音乐会，其中有一个由厦门毓德女中20名少女和寻源书院15名少年组成的混声合唱。受到学校流行弦乐队的启发，1925年，寻源书院那位1923年至1926年在华做事的教师乔治·科思牧师组织了一支有20件乐器的乐队，很快地就有许多人要求这支乐队到各个礼拜堂的聚会和城市公园的音乐会演奏。1926年，一场由33名学生和一支小乐队伴奏表演的合唱《明亮的星》，对中国公众乃是一次完全新的冒险尝试。演出过程中，其中有一座礼拜堂连走廊、窗户和进口处都挤满了人。

◎ 毓德女中第十五届音乐会留影。（白桦　供图）
The 15th Concert at Loktek Girls' School. (Courtesy of Bai Hua)

In 1906, Loktek Girls' School brought in a pipe organ from Europe for the choir. Transported all the way to Kulangsu, the organ was kept in the Gospel Chapel of Christian Church at Yanzijiao for the accompaniment of the choir. Uniquely shaped, it stood as tall as a person, and required two people to play, with one person blowing, and the other pressing keys. This curious instrument was once a unique attraction of the island.

In 1913, Lin Erjia (Lim Nee Kar), owner of Shuzhuang Garden as well as a rich islander from Taiwan, bought a real piano from Europe, and used it as home decor. This was the first piano on Kulangsu. Since then, wealthy businessmen on the island followed suit and bought pianos, as well as Trinity Church and missionary schools. The number of pianos on the island increased gradually until it was the highest per capita in China. Indeed, it was rare even across the world to have such a large number of pianos concentrated in such a small place. In the 1920s and 1930s, Western music had been very popular on Kulangsu which made the island a well-known "music island" at home and abroad.

Church activities usually involved a choir performance accompanied by the piano. Missionary schools offered classes in hymn singing and often held performance competitions. Music also became a popular extra-curricular activity in schools and often served as a unique means contributing to the Gospel of Revelation. A unique entertainment program for the Chinese was presented at the 1921 Christmas concert, including a mixed chorus of 20 girls from Loktek Girls' School and 15 boys from Xunyuan Academy. Another story had it that inspired by the school's popular string band, Rev. George Kots, a teacher of Xunyuan Academy who worked in China from 1923 to 1926, organized a band with 20 instruments in 1925, and soon it was invited to play in various church congregations and concerts in city parks. It was said that in 1926, a chorus of *Twinkling Stars* performed by 33 students and a small band was an entirely new experience for the Chinese public. During the performance, the hallways, windowsills and entrances were all crowded with people.

20世纪30年代中期，鼓浪屿上女子中学对小学音乐教师和礼拜堂合唱队指挥的培养都十分用心。《归正教在中国》一书中提到一位出色的美国女钢琴家敏戈登太太，著名的钢琴教育家李嘉禄便是她的学生，她从1917年随丈夫来到鼓浪屿后，除太平洋战争那几年外，一直在岛上指导音乐活动，或为演唱伴奏，或组织合唱团演出，还帮助毓德女子中学的一支管弦乐队使用唯一的中国乐器。

　　因为学校音乐教育的普及，百姓积极参与的教会活动——三一堂唱诗班（有歌颂团、青年诗班、少年诗班、儿童诗班）在海内外都颇有影响。教会组织了歌剧班、戏剧班、声乐班、钢琴班、风琴班、口琴班、西乐研究班等，成立了"声影剧社"和歌咏团，不时举办音乐会。鼓浪屿上音乐爱好者日众，他们不仅懂得欣赏，更学会了弹唱。

　　岛上音乐活动频繁而活跃：20世纪30年代，国民党军委军乐队曾来岛上举行音乐会；小提琴家尼哥罗、男高音歌唱家陈玄等也来此举行音乐会。而当时居住在岛上的留英的厦门大学校长林文庆，留美的厦门自来水公司总工程师林全诚等都时常互相以音乐交流，使小岛上音乐气氛浓厚。

　　1948年7月，林克恭在鼓浪屿创办厦门艺术协会，这以后大约每半个月他便在家里举办一次音乐会，邀请爱好音乐的友人来家中作客，开创了鼓浪屿家庭音乐会的先河。后来，大提琴手廖永廉、钢琴手阮鸣凤、小提琴手储耀武、男高音温绍杰等都在家里不定期地举行过音乐会。家庭音乐会成为岛上音乐爱好者家庭的高雅娱乐，这些家庭亦成为岛上的音乐世家，后代中培养出许多音乐家。

◎ 三一堂会吟诗团。（白桦 供图）
Singing choir of Trinity Church. (Courtesy of Bai Hua)

In the mid-1930s, girls' schools on Kulangsu attached great importance to the training of music teachers for primary schools and conductors for chapel choirs. The book *The Reformed Church in China* made mention of an excellent American female pianist Stella Veenschoten, whose student Li Jialu later became a well-known piano educator. From 1917, when she came to Kulangsu with her husband, she was committed to guiding music events on the island, accompanying singing, or organizing chorus performances except during the Pacific War. She also taught the orchestra at Loktek Girls' School how to use the only Chinese musical instrument they had.

The popularity of music education in schools drew more and more local islanders to take active part in church activities. For instance, Trinity Church had its own singing choir, youth choir, teenage choir and children's choir. These choirs had quite an impact at home and abroad at the time. The church organized classes in opera, drama, vocal music, piano, pipe organ, harmonica, and Western music. A film & drama club and singing group were set up to hold regular concerts. The number of music lovers on Kulangsu was on the rise and they learnt not only how to appreciate music, but also how to sing and play the instruments.

There were regular musical events on the island. In the 1930s, a band from the Kuomintang Military Commission once came to the island to hold concerts, as did violinist Niccolo and tenor Chen Xuan. Lim Boon Keng (Lin Wenqing), then president of Amoy University who once studied in Britain, often went to such concerts with his friend Lin Quancheng, chief engineer of Amoy Water Supply Company who returned from the US, when they lived on the island. All these added to the musical atmosphere on Kulangsu.

In July 1948, artist Lin Kegong founded the Amoy Art Association on Kulangsu and had since held a concert in his house approximately every fortnight, inviting music-loving friends as guests, marking the beginning of family concerts on the island. Later, musicians like cellist Liao Yonglian, pianist Ruan Mingfeng, violinist Chu Yaowu, tenor Wen Shaojie and others held family concerts in their own houses at different times. This practice has been passed down as a venue for entertainment and a pastime for the island's music loving families, helping to foster many musicians from later generations.

◎ 著名花腔女高音颜宝玲。（白桦 供图）
Distinguished coloratura soprano Yan Baoling. (Courtesy of Bai Hua)

　　鼓浪屿的音乐传统根基深厚，也令岛上的居民深深怀念。舒婷的笔下曾经写过这样一个岛上典型的音乐家庭："当我们看到廖先生打起黑领结，扛着扬名四十年代的大提琴，便知道今晚哪里该有家庭音乐会了（他所收藏的录音带之丰富完整，连央视都来做过专题。顺便说一句，年轻时的廖娘在基督教青年会合唱团里，也有一副让人怀念的女高音）。"

　　鼓浪屿的过去以及现在有过多少灿若星辰的名字，这些名字里有许多与音乐相关：如音乐教育家周淑安教授，她创作了中国第一首花腔歌曲《安眠曲》，这首歌是用厦门的方言童谣"呵呵困，一暝大一寸；呵呵惜，一暝大一尺"来反复吟唱八遍，配以钢琴伴奏；声乐家林俊卿教授；著名的花腔女高音颜宝玲；音乐理论家杨民望；著名钢琴演奏家殷承宗；钢琴教育家李嘉禄教授；大提琴演奏家陈鼎臣教授；旅美钢琴家许斐平、许斐星、许兴艾；著名指挥家陈佐煌；手风琴、钢琴演奏家兼教育家李未明……

The deep-rooted musical tradition on Kulangsu is lovingly integrated into the local community. Shu Ting once wrote about one of the island's typical musician families: "Whenever we saw Mr. Liao wearing a black bow tie and carrying his cello of the 1940s, we knew there would be a family concert in the evening somewhere. He has had such a rich and complete collection of tapes that even China's Central Television came to him for a special feature program. By the way, Mrs. Liao used to be a member of the YMCA choir when she was young and has also got a soprano voice remembered by many."

Indeed, Kulangsu has been the birthplace in the past and present for a plethora of famous people, many of whom have been China's most accomplished musicians, including Professor Zhou Shu'an, a musician and educator who wrote and composed China's first coloratura *A Lullaby*, a nursery rhyme in Amoy vernacular which chanted "Sleep, sleep to grow, taller and taller with good sleeps" eight times, with piano accompaniment; vocalist and professor Lin Junqing; distinguished coloratura soprano Yan Baoling; music theorist Yang Minwang; famous pianist Yin Chengzong; piano educator and professor Li Jialu; cellist and professor Chen Dingchen; visiting pianists in the US such as Xu Feiping, Xu Feixing and Xu Xing'ai; famous conductor Chen Zuohuang and accordion, piano player and educator Li Weiming, to mention a few.

◎ 著名钢琴演奏家殷承宗。（白桦 供图）
Famous pianist Yin Chengzong. (Courtesy of Bai Hua)

◎ 鼓浪屿钢琴博物馆。（鼓浪屿钢琴博物馆 供图）
Kulangsu Piano Museum. (Courtesy of Kulangsu Piano Museum)

音乐之岛的爱与希望

　　出生在鼓浪屿的音乐家、收藏家胡友义，晚年在故乡建起了中国第一个钢琴博物馆——鼓浪屿钢琴博物馆。鼓浪屿钢琴博物馆选址在当年拥有鼓浪屿第一台钢琴的菽庄花园"听涛轩"，是当时亚洲最大、全国唯一的钢琴博物馆。

　　钢琴博物馆内收藏了100多架来自世界各国的名古钢琴和百盏古钢琴灯台：克莱门蒂19世纪初制造的世界上最大、音响最为洪亮的四角钢琴，钢琴制造大师舒楠1906年制作的有4套琴弦、8个踏板、两层琴键且黑白琴键颠倒的双键盘古钢琴，勃德制于1878年、琴腿为"S"形的钢琴，街头艺人卖艺的手摇街头钢琴，1928年美国制造、价格昂贵的全自动"海那斯"名琴，以及出生在鼓浪屿的钢琴教育家李嘉禄教授一生所钟爱的德国柏林20世纪初制造的三角钢琴……为了音乐之岛的延续，胡友义夫妇无偿捐献毕生所藏，让涛声与琴音共鸣。

Passion and Hope on the "Island of Music"

Hu Youyi, a musician and collector born on the island, established Kulangsu Piano Museum in his ancestral home in his later years. Located in the building "Billows Sound" (Tingtao) in Shuzhuang Garden where the first piano on Kulangsu was housed, the museum was Asia's largest and China's first and the only piano museum at the time.

The piano museum has an impressive collection of more than 100 famous clavichords and lamp stands from all over the world, including a quadrangle crafted by Muzio Clementi, the world's largest and most sonorous piano made in the early 19th century; the clavichord with 4 sets of strings, 8 pedals, 2 layers of keys and reversed black and white keys made in 1906 by the piano manufacturer Schramm & Sons; the piano made in 1878 by Byrd with "S" shaped legs; a street musician's barrel piano; the expensive and fully automatic 1928 "Haines" made in the US and the grand piano made in Berlin in the early 20th century and favorite of professor Li Jialu, a piano educator born on Kulangsu. Hu Youyi and his wife donated their lifetime collections to enrich the legacy of the musical island and pass it down to future generations.

◎ 克莱门蒂钢琴。（鼓浪屿钢琴博物馆 供图）
Clementi. (Courtesy of Kulangsu Piano Museum)

钢琴博物馆建成后，胡友义决定再建一座风琴博物馆。位于鼓浪屿地标建筑八卦楼的鼓浪屿风琴博物馆是中国唯一、世界最大的专门展示古风琴的博物馆。博物馆内收藏有各类风琴60多架（台）。1909年出厂的5米高、3米多宽、有着1,350根音管的英国诺曼·比尔德管风琴在八卦楼的穹顶下被奏响时，整座八卦楼里响彻着它的乐声，庄重宏雅。

风琴博物馆的镇馆之宝——卡萨翁第700号管风琴，1917年诞生于波士顿。2007年，胡友义从美国波士顿拍卖会上购得这架管风琴。卡萨翁第700号管风琴被誉为北美四大名琴之一，整架琴高达13米，宽12.5米，重35吨，有144个音栓、7,451根音管、4层手键盘，是目前国内最大的管风琴。历时三年的修复之后，2018年卡萨翁第700号管风琴在专门为它量身修建的鼓浪屿管风琴艺术中心亮相，并请来巴黎圣母院主管风琴师拉特利举行独奏音乐会，庆贺这架名琴诞生百年的重生。

除了随时可到这些专业的音乐展馆与琴音相遇，岛上的居民们依然时常举办家庭音乐会，比如成员们都不年轻的"雷厝乐队"还很活跃，也许音乐才使他们激情不老，永远年轻。当然，也可以到音乐厅听一场免费的音乐会，还可以在每一年的"音乐周"上"邂逅"受邀而来的音乐名家。

琴声如诉，这座岛屿最悠长最值得回味的故事，一定和音乐有关。

◎ 卡萨翁第700号管风琴。（朱庆福 摄）
Casavant Opus 700 pipe organ. (Photo by Zhu Qingfu)

After the completion of the piano museum, Hu Youyi decided to build an organ museum. Located in the landmark Bagua Mansion (Eight Trigrams Mansion), Kulangsu Organ Museum was the only in China and the largest in the world for the display of ancient organs. There are more than 60 organs in the museum, including the five-meter-high, three-meter-wide British "Norman & Beard" pipe organ made in 1909 with 1,350 tubes. When it was played under the dome of Bagua Mansion, the whole building was filled with its grand sound.

The most impressive highlight of the museum is the Casavant Opus 700 pipe organ made in Boston in 1917, which Hu purchased from an auction in Boston in 2007. The giant organ is known as one of the four most famous organs in North America. Standing at 13 meters high, 12.5 meters wide and weighing 35 tons, the instrument is the largest pipe organ on the Chinese mainland so far with 144 stubs, 7,451 tubes and a four-tier keyboard. In 2018, after three years of restoration, the Casavant Opus 700 pipe organ was unveiled at the tailor-made new Kulangsu Pipe Organ Art Center, and Notre Dame's master organist Olivier Latry was invited to give a recital to celebrate the centenary of the organ's birthday.

In addition to the easy access to these professional music museums, residents of the island have been carrying on the tradition of holding family concerts. For example, "Lei's House Band" is still active with youthful passion although its members are no longer young. Of course, you may also go to one of the free concerts, or "encounter" accomplished musicians invited for the annual "Kulangsu Music Week".

The sound of music lingers and the island's long and memorable stories have much to do with its rich musical legacy.

◎ "雷厝乐队" 的街头音乐会。（康伦恩 摄）
Street music by Lei's House Band. (Photo by Kang Lun'en)

◎ 马约翰体育场。（杨戈 摄）
Ma Yuehan Stadium. (Photo by Yang Ge)

体育的百年传统

音乐是鼓浪屿的美妙元素，体育运动也是小岛值得骄傲的历史——除了"钢琴之岛"的美誉，鼓浪屿亦有"足球之岛"之称。

随着西人的脚步踏足鼓浪屿，各种当时国内罕见的西方近代体育运动也来到了鼓浪屿。据牛津大学出版的《中国赛马》一书记载，厦门开埠后，英军便在鼓浪屿修建了跑马场，并在1842年秋天举行了首次赛马，这是中国举办的首次赛马。

1876年，在鹿耳礁附近建起的万国俱乐部旁有一座小剧场和一座壁球馆。附近的"洋人球埔"（曾名"人民体育场"，现称"马约翰体育场"）是中国最早的足球场。它最初是鸦片战争期间英军开辟的军用操场，1870年前后，这片平坦的空地被美国驻厦门领事李礼让以美国领事馆名义租下，开辟为驻岛外国人进行体育活动的公众场所。"洋人球埔"曾作为草地网球、草地板球、羽毛球等体育活动项目的活动场地。后来随着美、英各国水兵的到访，场地又引入了足球、棒球、橄榄球等团体竞技项目。1903年，美国领事馆将其交由工部局代为管理。1909年至1911年间，居住在鼓浪屿的外国人还在这里举办过每年一届的家庭亲子运动会。1910年为欢迎美国商会代表团访问厦门，这里举行过足球、网球比赛等重要活动。

Centuries-Old Tradition of Sports

Much like music is a beautiful element of Kulangsu, sports also contribute to the proud history of the island. Adding to the reputation of "piano island", Kulangsu is also known as "football island".

Together with Westerners who set their foot on Kulangsu, a variety of modern sports were introduced to Kulangsu. According to the book *China Races* by Austin Coates published by Oxford University in 1983, as Amoy was opened as one of the treaty ports, the British army built a racecourse on Kulangsu and held the first horse race in the autumn of 1842, which was also the first in China.

In 1876, Amoy Club was established near Lu'erjiao. Next to the club were a small theatre and a squash court. Nearby was Foreigners' Football Field (once named People's Stadium and now Ma Yuehan Stadium), China's earliest football field, which was originally used as a military playground opened by the British army during the Opium War. Around 1870, the piece of flat vacant land was rented by Le Gendre, the US consul in Amoy, in the name of the American Consulate, and opened to the public as a sports ground for foreigners on the island. Foreigners' Football Field had been used as a venue for lawn tennis, lawn cricket, badminton and other sports. Later on, football, baseball, rugby and other team sports were introduced with visits of sailors from the United States and Britain. In 1903, the American Consulate put the field under the administration of the Kulangsu Municipal Council. Between 1909 and 1911, foreign islanders held annual family sports meetings on the site. In 1910, important events such as football and tennis matches were held to welcome the visiting delegation of American Chamber of Commerce to Amoy.

◎ 2016年"鼓浪屿"杯足球俱乐部友谊赛在马约翰体育场举办。（康伦恩 摄）
Friendship match of "Kulangsu Cup" Football Match held in Ma Yuehan Stadium in 2016. (Photo by Kang Lun'en)

◎ 英华足球队获1930年厦门足球公开比赛锦标纪念照。（白桦 供图）
Anglo-Chinese Football Team winning the 1930 Amoy Open Football Championship. (Courtesy of Bai Hua)

1897年，英国人开始在鼓浪屿燕尾山麓建造简易的高尔夫球场，开展高尔夫运动并举办单打和双打比赛，这里也成为中国最早的高尔夫球场之一。

19世纪末英国领事馆新馆建成后，领事官员开始将保龄球带入鼓浪屿，这是最早传入中国的保龄球。当时的保龄球有不同的材质和规格，可供成人和儿童娱乐，可用于室内或户外草坪。后来，保龄球活动从领事馆进入万国俱乐部，成为公共娱乐项目。

早期的教会学校会在课外开展一些健身活动。1890年，寻源书院把体格、画图和音乐定为必修的课程，体育开始成为一门学科。其他教会学校也先后开设了体育课。1898年，鼓浪屿的英国领事和一些绅士们向岛上的中学与男童小学赠送了一整套板球和足球，用以鼓励体育以及运动的发展。在教会创办的学校里，田径、篮球、足球、乒乓球、网球等西方近代体育项目或成为学生的必修课，或成为他们课余的活动。教会学校组织班级、学校篮球队、足球队，经常开展校内和校际的比赛活动，举行以田径为主的运动会或单项竞赛，还举办过校运会。

早在1890年，鼓浪屿就有足球运动的倡议。最初，英国传教士创办的英华书院的师生受此影响，也喜欢踢足球。英华书院于是率先引进了英国现代足球——1898年成立福建省第一支足球队，同时也是中国近代第一支足球队，这是厦门乃至福建足球运动之发端。《归正教在中国》一书中写道："1898年，英国传教士山雅各在鼓浪屿创办英华书院，这是鼓浪屿影响较大的西式学校。英华学院创办不久，即成立了英华足球队，这是中国近代史上第一支足球队。"英华书院的足球队曾出征外地，赢得不少声誉，比如1920年，他们作为省运会的冠军应邀前往香港比赛。

1902年，清政府规定各级新学堂都要设置体育课，近代西方的体育运动在鼓浪屿开始发展。就连女子学校也开设了体育课程。1920年，鼓浪屿还举行了首次女子篮球比赛。20世纪30年代，鼓浪屿有名目繁多的足球队、游泳队，每年都举办各种形式的足球赛和游泳比赛，对外体育交流频繁，英华足球队、波浪游泳队的战绩蜚声东南亚。

In 1897, the British began to build a golf course at the foot of Yanwei Hill on Kulangsu for exercises and matches. It was also one of the earliest golf courses in China.

At the end of the 19th century when the new British Consulate was built, bowling was brought to Kulangsu with the officers, which was also the first time bowling was introduced to China. The bowls were available in a variety of materials and sizes and bowling as an entertaining sport was suitable for both adults and children and could be played indoors or outdoors. Later, bowling moved out from the consulate to Amoy Club and became a public pastime.

Early missionary schools would carry out some fitness activities outside class. In 1890, Xunyuan Academy began to set body building, drawing and music as compulsory courses, and physical education became a discipline. Other missionary schools also introduced physical education classes. In 1898, the British consul on Kulangsu and some gentlemen presented a complete set of cricket and football to the island's secondary schools and boys' primary schools to encourage the development of sports. In the schools established by the church, athletics, basketball, football, table tennis, tennis and other modern Western sports became compulsory courses or extracurricular activities for students. Missionary schools organized classes, school basketball teams, football teams to go in for on-campus and inter-school sports competitions, holding athletic meets, individual events or school sports meetings.

As early as 1890, there was an initiative to bring football to Kulangsu. This was applauded by football-loving teachers and students from the Anglo-Chinese College (Yinghua Academy) established by British missionaries, which first introduced soccer. In 1898, the first football team in Fujian Province and in modern China was founded, marking the beginning of football in Amoy and Fujian. As described in the book *The Reformed Church in China*: "In 1898, the British missionary Rev. James Sadler founded Anglo-Chinese College on Kulangsu, which was a Western-style school with great influence on Kulangsu. Soon after its establishment, Anglo-Chinese Football Team was built, which was the first in the modern history of China." The football team won many awards from competitions and was invited to play in Hong Kong as the champion of the 1920 provincial games.

In 1902, the Qing Government stipulated that all levels of modern schools should offer PE classes, and modern Western sports began to develop on Kulangsu, including in girls' schools. In 1920, Kulangsu held the first women's basketball match. In the 1930s, Kulangsu boasted numerous football and swimming teams, and held all forms of football and swimming competitions every year, with frequent sports exchanges with the outside world. Anglo-Chinese Football Team and Waves Swimming Team were known far and wide in Southeast Asia.

厦门基督教青年会更将近现代体育运动推向社会。他们与厦门体育界合作，向体育爱好者教授足球、排球、篮球、网球和田径运动，并逐渐配备了相应的活动设施：他们建立足球队、篮球队、排球队、乒乓球队、网球队和游泳队，组织横渡厦鼓海峡（厦门岛与鼓浪屿岛之间海峡）和环鼓（环绕鼓浪屿）游泳赛、帆船赛、越野长跑赛、自行车长途赛和中国象棋赛等，举办体操、跳水、曲棍球、武术等训练。

鼓浪屿四面皆海，是天然的游泳场所。岛上的原住民以海为生，自然有水下本领，他们把下海游泳叫作"泅渡"。据说郑成功在岛上操练水兵，游泳便是主要训练科目。教会也适时地推出了游泳比赛。1931年9月5日，厦门基督教青年会在鼓浪屿田尾游泳场举办厦门第一届游泳比赛，这是福建最早的游泳比赛。1931年9月26日，厦门基督教青年会主办第一次横渡厦鼓海峡的泅渡比赛活动。

◎ 1932年毓德女中排球队参加厦门排球锦标赛。（白桦 供图）
Volleyball team of Loktek Girls' School at Amoy Volleyball Championship, 1932. (Courtesy of Bai Hua)

◎ 1933年鼓浪屿毓德女中学生做早操。（白桦 供图）
Girls at Loktek Girls' School doing morning exercises, 1933.(Courtesy of Bai Hua)

Amoy YMCA had a role to play in the introduction of modern sports to the community. They worked with Amoy sports circles to coach sports enthusiasts in ball games and track and field, and to provide corresponding facilities. They built teams in football, basketball, volleyball, table tennis, tennis and swimming. They also organized competitions such as swimming and sailing competitions across the strait between Amoy and Kulangsu or around the island, including cross-country running, long-distance cycling race and Chinese chess, among others. There were also training courses in gymnastics, diving, hockey and Wushu (martial arts).

Surrounded by the sea, Kulangsu is a natural site for swimming. Native islanders made a living by the sea and were endowed talent for swimming, a critical part of their daily life. It is said that swimming was a key training item when Koxinga trained his sailors on the island. The church had duly launched swimming competitions. On September 5, 1931, Amoy YMCA held the first swimming competition in Tianwei Bathing Beach, which was the earliest such event in Fujian. On September 26, 1931, the first swimming competition across the strait between Amoy and Kulangsu was held, hosted also by Amoy YMCA.

正是因为在同一时期超前的体育启蒙，鼓浪屿也出现了不少承继体育传统的名人。出生在鼓浪屿的马约翰，被誉为中国体坛宗师，正是他开创了中国近代体育教育之先河。马约翰在清华执教终生，许多学生都得益于他的体育教学：梁思成说自己"当年可是马约翰先生的好学生，有名的足球健将，在全校运动会上得过跳高第一名，单双杠和爬绳的技巧也是呱呱叫的……我非常感谢马约翰。想当年如果没有一个好身体，怎么搞野外调查？在学校中单双杠和爬绳的训练，使我后来在测绘古建筑时，爬梁上柱攀登自如"。现在，"马约翰杯"运动会已经成为清华大学一年一度的最高体育赛事。

1936年10月，马约翰还曾担任中国参加在柏林举行的第十一届世界奥林匹克运动会代表团总教练。

在体育的星空里熠熠生辉的鼓浪屿人，还有原北京体育学院院长马启伟；上海体育学院院长陈安槐；第一支出国征战的女子篮球队队长邵锦英；多次获得全国女子蛙泳冠军，并多次创全国纪录，被时人誉为"女蛙王"的蔡美玲；曾经获得国际女子游泳比赛冠军的傅翠美等。

如今马约翰的塑像正对着当年的"洋人球埔"，鸡蛋花落满了小广场。如果恰巧遇见体育场内有孩童踢球，笑声朗朗，似乎可以看到百年的历史更迭，过去与现在重合，回望开始，尚未结束。

◎ 毓德女子学校获1932年思明排球、篮球冠军。（白桦 供图）

Loktek Girls' School winning Siming volleyball and basketball matches in 1932. (Courtesy of Bai Hua)

Thanks to all this sports being introduced during this period of time, Kulangsu had turned out quite a number of accomplished figures to the sporting world. For instance, Ma Yuehan, born on Kulangsu, was reputed as the "grandmaster of Chinese sports" owing to his ground-breaking contributions to modern PE education in China. He spent his lifetime teaching sports in Tsinghua University and many students benefited from him. Liang Sicheng, a renowned Chinese architect, once said, "I used to be one of the good students of Mr. Ma Yuehan, and a popular football player. I won the first prize in high jump at the school sports meet and was doing very well in parallel and single bars and rope climbing... I'm very grateful to Ma Yuehan. If I hadn't got a healthy and strong body, how could I do my field research? Thanks to the school training in bars and rope climbing, I was later able to climb up beams and columns easily when I was mapping ancient buildings." Now, the "Ma Yuehan Cup" Sports Meet has become the most prestigious annual sports event of Tsinghua University.

In October 1936, Ma Yuehan acted as the head coach of the Chinese delegation to the 11th World Olympic Games in Berlin.

The abundance of outstanding sports people from Kulangsu also include Ma Qiwei, former President of Beijing Institute of Physical Education; Chen Anhuai, President of Shanghai Institute of Physical Education; Shao Jinying, captain of the first women's basketball team competing abroad; Cai Meiling, winner of many national women's breaststroke championships and setter of quite a few national records and therefore dubbed "Breaststroke Queen"; and Fu Cuimei, who won a gold medal in an international women's swimming competition.

Today in the small square scattered with falling petals of red-jasmine stands the statue of Ma Yuehan overlooking former Foreigners' Football Field. If you happen to see children playing football in the stadium, full of joy and laughter, you may have the feeling that what started a hundred years ago is and will be going on, year after year and generation after generation.

◎ 马约翰与学生在一起。（白桦 供图）
Ma Yuehan and his students. (Courtesy of Bai Hua)

◎ 2013年第五届厦门鼓浪屿十人制橄榄球赛。（康伦恩 摄）
The 5th Ten-A-Side Rugby Match, Kulangsu, Amoy, 2013. (Photo by Kang Lun'en)

○3
旅行规划及其他信息

旅行规划

经典游一日线路

　　三丘田码头遗址→美国领事馆旧址→私立鼓浪屿医院及宏宁医院旧址→船屋→鼓浪屿工部局遗址→《重兴鼓浪屿三和宫记》摩崖石刻→八卦楼（鼓浪屿风琴博物馆）→汇丰银行公馆旧址→汇丰银行职员公寓旧址→祈祷岩→许斐星、许斐平旧居→春草堂→观彩楼→亦足山庄→林文庆旧居→鼓浪屿会审公堂旧址→三一堂→日光岩景区（西林·瞰青别墅，日光岩寺，郑成功纪念馆）→英国伦敦差会女传教士宅（姑娘楼）→林屋→殷承宗旧居→基督教会墓园→安献楼→拼音小路→美华沙滩→鼓浪石→菽庄花园（鼓浪屿钢琴博物馆）→丹麦大北电报公司旧址→厦门海关验货员公寓旧址→洋人球埔（马约翰体育场）→廖家别墅（林语堂故居）→鼓浪屿电话公司旧址→中南银行旧址

深度游主题线路

■ 一、万国建筑之旅

美国领事馆旧址→海关理船厅公所旧址→海关通讯塔旧址→救世医院和护士学校旧址→船屋→鼓浪屿工部局遗址→八卦楼→杨家园→蒙学堂旧址（吴添丁阁）→番婆楼→三一堂→黄赐敏别墅（金瓜楼）→大夫第→四落大厝→英商亚细亚火油公司旧址→黄家花园→黄氏小宗→延平戏院旧址→廖家别墅（林语堂故居）→李家庄→白宅→英国领事公馆旧址→海天堂构→怡园→黄荣远堂→李传别别墅→容谷→林氏府及小八角楼→许家园→日本领事馆旧址→日本警察署及宿舍旧址→天主堂→西班牙领事馆旧址→协和礼拜堂→博爱医院旧址→海滨旅社

■ 二、宗教怀旧之旅

救世医院和护士学校旧址→《重兴鼓浪屿三和宫记》摩崖石刻→祈祷岩→日光岩寺→英国伦敦差会女传教士宅（姑娘楼）→安礼逊牧师楼→安献楼→基督教会墓园→拼音小路→种德宫→三一堂→怀仁女校（人民小学）→怀德幼稚园（日光幼儿园）→西欧小筑→英华书院（厦门二中）→蒙学堂（吴添丁阁）→福民小学→毓德女学堂→怜儿堂→三落姑娘楼→兴贤宫→复兴堂→天主堂→协和礼拜堂→闽南圣教书局旧址

■ 三、博物馆、纪念馆之旅

鼓浪屿历史文化陈列馆（英国领事馆旧址）→中国唱片博物馆（黄荣远堂）→林巧稚纪念馆（毓园）→马约翰纪念馆（荷兰领事馆旧址）→郑成功纪念馆→鼓浪屿钢琴博物馆（菽庄花园听涛轩）→鼓浪屿风琴博物馆（八卦楼）→故宫鼓浪屿外国文物馆（救世医院旧址）

Tours Recommended and Other Information

Tours Recommended

Classical Day-Trip Tour

Former site of Sanqiutian Jetty→Former American Consulate→Former Private Kulangsu Hospital & Hongning Hospital→Boat House→Former site of Kulangsu Municipal Council→Cliff Inscriptions about Sanhe Temple's Reconstruction→Bagua Mansion (Kulangsu Organ Museum)→Former Residence of HSBC'S President →Former Staff Residence of HSBC→Prayer Rock→Former House of Xu Feixing and Xu Feiping→Chuncao Villa→Guancai (Rainbow View) Building→Yizu Villa (Villa of Contentment)→Former House of Lim Boon Keng→Former Kulangsu Mixed Court→Trinity Church→Sunlight Rock Scenic Area (including Xilin Villa & Kanqing Villa, Sunlight Rock Temple and Koxinga Memorial)→Former Residence of London Missionary Society for Women (The Ladies' House)→Lin's House→Former House of Yin Chengzong→Cemetery of Christian Church→Anxian Hall→Pinyin Road→Meihua Beach→Drum Wave Rock→Shuzhuang Garden Villa (Kulangsu Piano Museum)→Former Office of Great Northern Telegraph Company (Denmark)→Former Amoy Customs Inspectors' Quarters→Former Foreigners' Football Field (Ma Yuehan Stadium)→Liao Family Villa (Former House of Lin Yutang)→Former Office of Kulangsu Telephone Company→Former China & South Sea Bank Limited

In-Depth Theme Tours

■ Option 1—Architecture of the World

Former American Consulate→Former Amoy Maritime Affairs Office→Former Amoy Customs Communication Tower→Former Hope Hospital and the Nurses' School→Boat House→Former site of Kulangsu Municipal Council→Bagua Mansion→Yang Family Mansion→Former Mengxuetang (Wu Tianding's Mansion)→Fanpo Mansion→Trinity Church→Huang Cimin Villa ("Golden Pumpkin" Building)→Dafudi Mansion→Four-Compound Mansion→Former Office Building of the British Asiatic Petroleum Company→Huang Family Villa→Huang's Ancestral Hall→Former Yanping Complex→Liao Family Villa (Former House of Lin Yutang)→Li Family Mansion→Bai Family House→Former British Consulate→Hai Tian Tang Gou Mansion→Yiyuan Garden→Huang Rongyuan Mansion→Li Chuanbie Villa→Banyan Valley Villa→Lin's House and Octagonal Building →Xu Family Villa→Former Japanese Consulate→Former Japanese Police Station and Staff Quarters→Catholic Church→Former Spanish Consulate→Union Church→Former Pok Oi Hospital→Seaside Hotel

■ Option 2—Religious Destinations

Former Hope Hospital and the Nurses' School→Cliff Inscriptions about Sanhe Temple's Reconstruction→Prayer Rock→Sunlight Rock Temple→Former Residence of London Missionary Society for Women(The Ladies' House)→Rev. J.N. Anderson Building→Anxian Hall→Cemetery of Christian Church→Pinyin Road→Zhongde (Virtue Cultivating) Temple→Trinity Church→Hoaijin (Huairen) Girls' School (People's Primary School)→Huaide Nursery(Sunlight Kindergarten)→Western-style Building→Anglo-Chinese College or Yinghua Academy (Xiamen No. 2 High School)→Former Mengxuetang (Wu Tianding's Mansion)→Fumin Primary School→Former Loktek Girls' School→Foundling Home→Three-Compound Ladies' House→Xingxian Temple→ Renaissance Church→Catholic Church→Union Church→Former Bookstore of South Fukien Religious Tract Society

■ Option 3—Museums and Memorials

Kulangsu Museum of History and Culture (Former British Consulate)→China Record Museum (Huang Rongyuan Mansion)→Lin Qiaozhi Memorial (Yuyuan Garden)→Ma Yuehan Memorial (Former Dutch Consulate)→Koxinga Memorial→Kulangsu Piano Museum ("Billows Sound" Building in Shuzhuang Garden)→Kulangsu Organ Museum (Bagua Mansion)→Kulangsu Gallery of Foreign Artifacts from the Palace Museum Collection (Former Hope Hospital)

博物馆、纪念馆等

■ 鼓浪屿历史文化陈列馆

地址：鹿礁路16号（英国领事馆旧址）

展馆突出了对鼓浪屿的导览功能，可通过展馆了解遍布鼓浪屿全岛的文化遗产。

门票：免票

开放时间：9:00—17:00

讲解服务时间：9:30、10:30、14:30、15:30、16:30

■ 中国唱片博物馆

地址：福建路32号（黄荣远堂）

中国唱片博物馆是国家级综合性唱片主题博物馆，馆内可以聆听到很多珍贵的历史声音，比如人类留音第一声、由爱迪生所哼唱的《玛丽有只小羊》等；还有不乏学术研究价值和收藏价值极高的镇馆之宝，比如"编钟之王"曾侯乙编钟出土后唯一一次演奏录音唱片《千古绝响》；1908年第一张在鼓浪屿录制的南音唱片等。

门票：68元/人

开放时间：9:00—17:30

■ 林巧稚纪念馆（毓园）

地址：复兴路102号

林巧稚是中国现代妇产科学的主要开拓者、奠基人之一。厦门市政府于1984年5月修建此园，纪念这位鼓浪屿的优秀女儿。

门票：免票

开放时间：

上午：8:15—11:30

下午：12:30—18:15（夏季）　12:30—17:45（冬季）

（周一闭馆）

■ 马约翰纪念馆

地址：中华路5号（荷兰领事馆旧址）

以纪念中国体育事业开拓者马约翰先生为主题的公益展览馆。

门票：免票

开放时间：

上午：8:15—11:30

下午：12:30—18:15（夏季）　12:30—17:45（冬季）（周一闭馆）

讲解服务时间：9:00、10:00、11:00、15:00、16:00

■ **郑成功纪念馆**

地址：永春路73号（日光岩景区内）

建于1962年，为纪念郑成功收复台湾300周年而建立。全馆分为7个部分，展出各种文物、资料、照片、雕塑、模型300余件，比较系统地展示了郑成功的生平事迹。

门票：包含在日光岩景区门票内

开放时间：8:30—17:00（周一闭馆）

■ **鼓浪屿钢琴博物馆**

地址：港后路7号（菽庄花园内）

建于2000年1月，是一家专门展示世界各国名古钢琴的专业博物馆。馆内展示了出生于鼓浪屿、旅居澳大利亚的钢琴收藏家胡友义先生毕生收藏的一百多架世界名古钢琴和百盏古钢琴灯台。

门票：包含在菽庄花园门票内

开放时间：8:15—18:15（夏季）8:15—17:45（冬季）

讲解服务时间：

一馆：9:00、10:00、11:00、13:30、14:30、15:30、16:30（讲解前后有自动钢琴演示）

二馆：9:30、10:30、11:30、14:00、15:00、16:00、17:00（讲解前后有钢琴演奏）

■ **鼓浪屿风琴博物馆**

地址：鼓新路43号（八卦楼）

国内唯一、世界最大的风琴博物馆。生产于1909年的一架风琴诺曼·比尔德为镇馆之宝之一。

门票：20元/人

开放时间：8:15—18:15（夏季）8:15—17:45（冬季）

讲解服务时间：9:30、10:30、11:30、12:30、14:00、15:00、16:00、17:00

■ **故宫鼓浪屿外国文物馆**

地址：鼓新路80号（救世医院旧址）

故宫鼓浪屿外国文物馆展示了故宫博物院收藏的明清两代遗存至今的外国文物。展品品类丰富、保存完整，不仅具有很高的艺术价值，更是中外文化交流的见证。

门票：50元/人

开放时间：周二至周日 9:00—17:00

（16:30停止售票，法定节假日和寒暑假周一也开放）

讲解服务时间：9:30、10:30、11:30、13:30、14:30、15:30

Museums and Memorials

■ Kulangsu Museum of History and Culture

Address: 16 Lujiao Road (Former British Consulate)

Featuring guided tours, the museum is an ideal destination where visitors can get a general idea about cultural heritage sites on Kulangsu.

Admission : Free

Opening : 9:00—17:00

Guided tours : 9:30, 10:30, 14:30, 15:30, 16:30

■ China Record Museum

Address: 32 Fujian Road (Huang Rongyuan Mansion)

China Record Museum is an integrated national theme museum, which holds a marvelous collection of precious historical voices, such as the first recording of human voice "Mary Had a Little Lamb", a nursery rhyme sung by Thomas Alva Edison. There are also many other treasures with high academic and collection value, such as the only recording of "Ancient Chinese Chimes" made after Zeng Houyi Chime, "King of Chimes" of the Warring States period over 2,400 years ago, was unearthed, as well as the first Nanyin music gramophone record made on Kulangsu in 1908.

Ticket: 68 *yuan*/person

Opening : 9:00—17:30

■ Lin Qiaozhi Memorial (Yuyuan Garden)

Address: 102 Fuxing Road

Lin Qiaozhi is one of the major pioneers and founders of modern obstetrics and gynecology in China and Xiamen Municipal Government built the garden in May 1984 to honor this outstanding daughter of Kulangsu.

Admission : Free

Opening: 8:15—11:30   12:30—18:15 (summertime)

　　　　　8:15—11:30   12:30—17:45 (wintertime)

　　　　(Closed on Mondays)

■ Ma Yuehan Memorial

Address: 5 Zhonghua Road (Former Dutch Consulate)

A public welfare theme exhibition, this is built in memory of Chinese sports pioneer Mr. Ma Yuehan.

Admission : Free

Opening : 8:15—11:30   12:30—18:15 (summertime)

          8:15—11:30   12:30—17:45 (wintertime)

        (Closed on Mondays)

Guided tours: 9:00, 10:00, 11:00, 15:00, 16:00

■ Koxinga Memorial

Address: 73 Yongchun Road (Within Sunlight Rock Scenic Area)

Built in 1962 to commemorate the 300th anniversary of Koxinga's recovery of Taiwan, the museum is divided into seven sections, displaying more than 300 pieces of cultural relics, documents, photos, sculptures and models, which showcases different aspects of the life of Koxinga.

Ticket: Included in ticket for Sunlight Rock Scenic Area

Opening: 8:30—17:00 (Closed on Mondays)

■ Kulangsu Piano Museum

Address: 7 Ganghou Road (Within Shuzhuang Garden)

Built in January of 2000, this is a theme museum showcasing all kinds of clavichords from different countries in the world. The impressive collection of more than 100 accompanying clavichords and lamp stands were donated by Hu Youyi, a piano collector who was born on Kulangsu and lived in Australia.

Ticket: Included in ticket for Shuzhuang Garden

Opening: 8:15—18:15 (summertime)

       8:15—17:45 (wintertime)

Guided tours:

Exhibition Hall 1: 9:00, 10:00, 11:00, 13:30, 14:30, 15:30, 16:30

       (Player piano playing before and after)

Exhibition Hall 2: 9:30, 10:30, 11:30, 14:00, 15:00, 16:00, 17:00

       (Piano playing before and after)

■ Kulangsu Organ Museum

Address: 43 Guxin Road (Bagua Mansion)

The organ museum is the only in China and the largest in the world, with the hugest "Norman & Beard" pipe organ made in 1909 as one of the highlights of the museum.

Ticket: 20 *yuan*/person

Opening: 8:15—18:15 (summertime)

　　　　8:15—17:45 (wintertime)

Guided tours: 9:30, 10:30, 11:30, 12:30, 14:00, 15:00, 16:00, 17:00

■ Kulangsu Gallery of Foreign Artifacts from the Palace Museum Collection

Address: 80 Guxin Road (Former Hope Hospital)

This spectacular new branch of the Palace Museum in Beijing showcases the museum's collection of foreign cultural relics from the Ming and Qing dynasties. The rich and well-preserved exhibits not only have high artistic value, but also bear witness to the cultural exchanges between China and other countries.

Ticket: 50 *yuan*/person

Opening: 9:00—17:00, Tuesday to Sunday

　　　　(Last admission at 16:30. Open also on Monday during statutory holidays and vacations)

Guided tours: 9:30, 10:30, 11:30, 13:30, 14:30, 15:30

食、住等推荐

■ 小憩推荐

褚家园咖啡（建于1932年的褚家园老别墅）

地址：中华路15号

城岸咖啡（八卦楼对面）

地址：鼓新路23号

汇丰银行公馆咖啡馆

（建于1870年代的汇丰银行公馆）

地址：鼓新路57号

■ 美食推荐

味友鸭肉面线（厦门老字号餐饮名店）

地址：龙头路菜市场2楼

捞海坞餐厅（朴素老宅里的闽南菜）

地址：乌埭路35号

再生海餐厅（主打清淡家常的海鲜菜肴）

地址：鼓新路9号

一口本垟菜（老别墅里的复古风格私房菜餐厅）

地址：安海路59号

邵子牙贡丸店（闽南老字号）

地址：龙头路178号

叶氏麻糍

地址：龙头商业街小广场

黄胜记肉松肉干（厦门百年老字号）

地址：龙头路95号

金兰饼店

地址：内厝澳413号

■ 住宿推荐

鼓山栖（鼓浪屿的百年老别墅钻石楼）

地址：鼓山路7号

黑檀（"淘化大同"创始合伙人黄廷元的老宅）

地址：鼓新路23号

漫漫悠悠（隐在内厝澳巷子里的百年老别墅）

地址：内厝澳100号

喜林阁（"姑娘楼"，鼓浪屿最古老的建筑之一）

地址：鸡山路1号

万水千山民宿（笔架山上的英式建筑）

地址：鼓新路33号

船屋老别墅旅馆（建于1920年的船屋）

地址：鼓新路48号

Food, Drink and Accommodation Recommendations

■ Coffee Breaks

Chu's Villa Café (Chu's old villa built in 1932)

Address: 15 Zhonghua Road

Citiark Coffee (Opposite Bagua Mansion)

Address: 23 Guxin Road

Café of Former Residence of HSBC's President
(Built in the 1870s)

Address: 57 Guxin Road

■ Delicacy Recommendations

Gourmet Thread Noodles in Duck Soup (An established restaurant in Xiamen)

Address: Second Floor, Food Market, Longtou Road

Food from the Sea (Old restaurant offering typical South Fujian cuisine)

Address: 35 Wudai Road

Sea on the Land (Featuring light seafood)

Address: 9 Guxin Road

A Bite of Local Delicacies (Vintage-style private home restaurant in an old villa)

Address: 59 Anhai Road

Shao Ziya's Meatballs (Old establishment in South Fujian)

Address: 178 Longtou Road

Ye's Glutinous Dumpling

Address: High Street Piazzetta, Longtou Road

Huangsheng's Meat Floss and Tasajo (A century-old establishment of Xiamen)

Address: 95 Longtou Road

Golden Orchid Bakery

Address: 413 Neicuo'ao

■ Accommodation Recommendations

Drum Rock Inn ("Diamond Villa", a one-hundred-year-old house)

Address: 7 Gushan Road

Rosewood Inn (The former house of Huang Tingyuan, one of the founding partners of "Amoy Food Limited")

Address: 23 Guxin Road

Leisure & Pleasure Inn (A century-old mansion in one of the quiet back streets)

Address: 100 Neicuo'ao

Silly Girl Home Inn ("The Ladies' House", one of the oldest buildings on the island)

Address: 1 Jishan Road

Hills and Sea View Inn (A British-style architecture on Bijia Hill)

Address: 33 Guxin Road

Old Boathouse Villa (The boathouse built in 1920)

Address: 48 Guxin Road

特别推荐

■ 虫洞书店

地址：福建路34号（海天堂构之一）

位于百年老别墅里的书店，或许是老别墅重生最好的范例。2016年开业的虫洞书店，位于海天堂构别墅群中的一幢。书店一层收有目前最全的关于鼓浪屿、厦门、闽南人文的书籍三千余册，且还在进一步收集中。书店二层是美术馆，经常有关于鼓浪屿的人文艺术展览，以及定期开展各类讲座。

■ 外图书店

地址：中华路21号（英商亚细亚火油公司旧址）

因其窗洞特别像圆睁双眼的猫头鹰，鼓浪屿人又称其为"猫头鹰楼"，2016年变身为外图书店。书店共三层，一、二层为书籍陈列室，三层为文化沙龙活动区，还特别设置了一间儿童绘本室供孩童阅览。

Special Recommendations

■ X-Readspace（The Worm Hole Bookstore）

Address: 34 Fujian Road (Part of Hai Tian Tan Gou Mansion)

Located in one of the buildings of a century-old mansion, the bookstore is the excellent rebirth of an old mansion. Opened in 2016, the bookstore holds an amazing collection of over 3,000 books on its first floor about local cultures and people on Kulangsu, in Xiamen and South Fujian in general, and the collection is said to be growing. The second floor is an art gallery where regular art exhibitions and seminars are held.

■ Foreign Language Bookstore

Address: 21 Zhonghua Road (Former Office Building of British Asiatic Petroleum Company)

The old villa was otherwise called "the owl building" by locals because all its windows look exactly like owls with opened eyes. Converted into a foreign language bookstore in 2016, it has three storeys, with the first and the second floors for books, and the third floor for cultural seminars. There is also a special reading room of picture books for children.

索 引

Index